Virginia Woolf's *Between the Acts* and Jane Harrison's Con/spiracy

Studies in Modern Literature, No. 78

A. Walton Litz, General Series Editor

Professor of English
Princeton University

Carolyn G. Heilbrun, Consulting Editor

Avalon Foundation Professor in the Humanities
Columbia University

Daniel Mark Fogel, Consulting Editor

Professor of English
Louisiana State University
Editor, *Henry James Review*

Other Titles in This Series

Virginia Woolf's *Between the Acts* and Jane Harrison's Con/spiracy

by
Patricia Maika

U·M·I Research Press

Ann Arbor / London

Produced and distributed by
UMI Research Press
an imprint of
University Microfilms, Inc.
Ann Arbor, Michigan 48106

Library of Congress Cataloging in Publication Data

Maika, Patricia, 1929-
Virginia Woolf's Between the acts and Jane Harrison's
conspiracy.

(Studies in modern literature ; no. 78)
Revision of the author's thesis — Simon
Fraser University.
Bibliography: p.
Includes index.
1. Woolf, Virginia, 1882-1941. Between the acts.
2. Woolf, Virginia, 1882-1941 — Political and social views.
3. Woolf, Virginia, 1882-1941 — Sources. 4. Harrison,
Jane Ellen, 1850-1928. Ancient art and ritual.
5. Ritual in literature. 6. Creation (Literary,
artistic, etc.) 7. Feminism and literature. I. Title.
II. Series.
PR6045.072B4236 1987   823'.912   87-13897
ISBN 0-8357-1818-2 (alk. paper)

British Library CIP data is available

To the memory of my mother:

Margaret Lucy Pharo
1901–1965

Tell all the Truth but tell it slant
Success in circuit lies
Too bright for our infirm Delight
The Truth's superb surprise
As Lightning to the Children eased
With Explanation kind
The Truth must dazzle gradually
Or every man be blind.

Emily Dickinson, 1129

An action like the action of the "Antigone" of Sophocles, which turns upon the conflict between the heroine's duty to her brother's corpse and that of the laws of her country, is no longer one in which it is possible that we should feel a deep interest.

Matthew Arnold, Preface to *Poems*

We need new art forms. New forms are wanted, and if they aren't available, we might as well have nothing at all.

Chekhov, *The Seagull*

Contents

Introduction

Act One

Critical attention paid to the novels and short stories of Virginia Woolf has, until recently, focused more on the poetic, innovative and experimental style of the writing than on the complexities of the themes and the nature of the politics behind them. In writing *A Room of One's Own* (1929), her long discussion of the position of women in relation to writing and to formal education, Woolf showed her awareness of the expectations of the male critics and publishers who were the arbiters of literary taste and indirectly the sources of her income. In a 1933 letter to Dame Ethyl Smythe quoted by Adrienne Rich, Woolf writes of "having kept her own personality out of *A Room of One's Own* lest she not be taken seriously: 'how personal, so will they say, rubbing their hands with glee, women always are: *I even hear them as I write*' " (emphasis Rich's).[1] In the same letter she writes, "I forced myself to keep my own figure fictitious; legendary."[2] *Three Guineas* (1938), the direct and challenging statement of her politics, received, as Woolf feared, more attention from the critics for its personal tone and style than for its pacifist, feminist and socialist stance. As late as 1968 Herbert Marder writes of its shrill and neurotic tone and lack of humour.[3]

Yet Woolf's fiction—poetic, stylistically innovative and experimental in form—was not easily or immediately understood, either due to what Madeline Moore describes as "the myopia of the male reviewers," or because Woolf couched her opinions, criticisms and truths in words which only those readers of remarkable perception could understand.[4] She employed a palimpsestic style similar in some ways to the many-layered novels of the Brontës and the cryptic poetry of Emily Dickinson described by Sandra Gilbert and Susan Gubar in *The Madwoman in the Attic*.[5] And she spoke as she made Lily Briscoe the female artist in *To the Lighthouse* speak to her friend Mrs. Ramsey, "not in any language known to men."[6]

Recent feminist criticism, that is, criticism that requires an understanding of women's lives and history, has drawn attention to the many levels of meaning in Woolf's work. Berenice Carroll suggested in 1978, "In interpreting Woolf's novels, it is necessary to recognize that particularly in the more mature works, there is hardly a word without significance, and that the significance is often a well concealed political message."[7] It seems now that Woolf's words about words, spoken in a BBC radio talk in 1937 have significance for the contemporary feminist critics who are scrutinizing and reviewing her work:

> Words never make anything that is useful; and words are the only things that tell the truth and nothing but the truth. . . . [T]hey have so often proved that they hate being useful, that it is their nature not to express one single statement but a thousand possibilities—they have done this so often that at last, happily, we are beginning to face the fact. . . . It is because the truth they try to catch is many-sided, and they convey it by being themselves many-sided, flashing this way, then that. Thus they mean one thing to one person, another thing to another person; they are unintelligible to one generation, plain as a pikestaff to the next.[8]

If this generation is fortunate enough to understand Woolf's words plainly, we must also be aware of the task she left us of deciphering the hidden messages, the buried themes; of following the "serpentine" subtleties of the insinuations through the maze of artistic, stylistic and allusive technical brilliance in which many previous critics have either become lost or not dared to venture.[9]

The genius of Woolf's writing, the intricate tracery of allusion and symbolism in which every word expresses "a thousand possibilities" is nowhere better hidden and, strangely, nowhere more apparent than in *Between the Acts,* the novel published after her death in 1941. Written in Woolf's mature years, when she was between fifty and sixty, it seems to be the culmination of her literary work, and I think requires a criticism informed by an understanding of her reasons for telling it "slant" and of her strategies for doing so, as well as a realization that she, Virginia Woolf, the female artist, "fictitious; legendary" the detested "I . . . large and ugly" removed, stands at the heart of the novel.[10]

Between the Acts is a statement of her commitment to the development of a communal art: an art that will influence and change the course of history. Musically, visually and verbally art creates and controls the world. Woolf's perspective has shifted slightly from that of *Three Guineas,* a straightforward condemnation of capitalism under patriarchy. Then Woolf called for the voluntary dissociation of women from the politics inspired (if that is possible) by the "dried ideas" in the "sterile mind[s]" of men.[11] Patriotism, she felt, should be rejected by women in favor of the "real loyalties" of love. She quoted Antigone: " ' 'Tis not my nature to join in hating, but in loving.' "[12] In *Between the Acts* she sees beyond a time of separation and division to a different kind of world in which all living things speak in their own way to the perpetually observant artist whose lonely task is to strive to re/interpret, re/present, and never cease to re/create and to unveil for others, their truths which only *she* can see. Her success comes with the brief moment her audience is united in the perception of their common vision. She continues to struggle to produce new works so that the world will continue to change and will be kept from the danger of death.

Woolf's view that participation in art and literature by all classes of people was not only essential for unity and peace but crucial to survival, she states unequivocally in the paper "The Leaning Tower" that she read to the Worker's Educational Association at Brighton in May 1940, at the time she was writing *Between the Acts*. She criticises a group of contemporary poets—Stephen Spender, Cecil Day Lewis, W. H. Auden and Louis MacNeice among them—for their inability to communicate the truths of working class experience, because the language of their poetry merely reflects their uncertain position between "two worlds, one dying, the other struggling to be born." These writers lean, according to Woolf, from the ivory tower which, because of their privileged education, contains them, toward the common ground where they long to be "with the mass of humankind."[13] She herself did not accept critic Desmond McCarthy's judgment that she too occupied the tower, for she felt "four thousand five hundred and fifty pounds" (a year) closer to the ground than he, a well-paid journalist and reviewer.[14] Woolf urges working-class people to read, write and criticise literature to bridge the gulf between the separate worlds of the educated and the uneducated, and to accomplish the eventual merging of all classes. She supports a "system of free national education" whereby those destined, in her words, to mix with the dead, at public schools—she cites Winchester—can attend village schools and "mix with the living."[15] Politically radical as her opinions are, they had little effect at the time she voiced them.

So it is not really surprising that she emphasised her views in a different way, uttered her prophesies in fictional form, in the peculiarly distilled and concentrated style she had evolved over the years of her most prolific writing. At first it may seem that Woolf's cryptic style belies the urgency of her message, if indeed it is essential for the future vitality of the world. But the form of *Between the Acts* itself provides a verbal paradigm of her vision of the unity of all things in an economical prose style in which every word expresses "a thousand possibilities." She breaks words into syllables and reunites the syllables in other words; by making anagrams of well-known words she flashes one or many associative meanings before us. She relies on the sound of words as well as the sight of them to provoke our understanding. The sounds of birds and animals join with human voices, musical sounds and the noise of machines in a new language suitable for use in the modern world.

Woolf's idiosyncratic use of the language she inherited goes beneath words to become sub/versive and to overturn accepted forms. In addition she deliberately takes apart and manipulates, entirely for her own purposes, the accepted myths of many cultures told by writers as diverse as Plutarch and Richard Wagner, as though obtaining a kind of revenge for the overshadowing by patriarchal Olympus of earlier cults of goddess worship particularly in primitive Greece and ancient Egypt. Perhaps the most daring and certainly the most questionable of her activities, if we consider the proprietorial aspect of literary convention, is her unabashed commandeering of pieces from the works of other writers to use in her own fictional creation.

Virginia Woolf suffered from the indignity of having to take second place to other writers of her time. She was trivialised by male critics, and friends dismissed her. W. H. Mellers in 1937, reviewing *The Years* for *Scrutiny*—a journal notorious for its view that Woolf did not inhabit the real world of female experience—wrote slightingly of her "refinement," her "celebrated femininity," her "tepid Bloomsbury prose" and her "minute social world."[16] E. M. Forster, the friend with whom she got drunk one night, and who revealed that he, a homosexual, found "sapphism" disgusting for it made women independent of men, called her "cantankerous" and "old fashioned."[17]

Woolf was intensely critical of the writings of her contemporaries. She felt that they had no vision, no new plots for the world's continuance. She was "not a little jealous" of Lytton Strachey's success with *Eminent Victorians,* his witty iconoclastic version of nineteenth-century history which, although peppered with clichés and written in a sensational style, brought him fame, respect and a considerable amount of money.[18] Although she approved of Strachey mocking the Victorian age she found his work "too much afraid of dulness to say anything out of the way."[19] He irked her too by praising T. S. Eliot more effusively than she liked.[20] Eliot puzzled her for she recognized the importance of his poetry but disagreed with his religious views. She felt there was "something obscene in a living person sitting by the fire and believing in God."[21] Eliot's solution to the alienation of the twentieth century, his longing for the "perpetual star/Multifoliate rose" is very little different from Matthew Arnold's lament from the nineteenth century for the "Sea of Faith."[22] To the atheist Woolf, a proposal to return to Christian beliefs was another indication of the blind confidence of men in a paternalistic myth that could not show a new direction for humanity. She also resented Eliot's neglect of her as a writer and the condescending way he pronounced her short stories "very good" and James Joyce's *Ulysses* "prodigious."[23]

That Virginia Woolf disliked Joyce's *Ulysses* is well known. She was at first shocked by the language, but later, when she felt she saw the meaning, thought she might revise her views.[24] She concluded that *Ulysses* was a landmark because it destroyed the whole of the nineteenth century, but again felt it offered nothing new.[25] In short, Strachey satirised and mocked; Joyce shocked and dismayed; Eliot's vision was as depressing as his regressive solution of returning to the values of a male Christian god. Woolf's dissatisfaction with the writings of these, her contemporaries, is reflected to some extent in her writing of *Between the Acts.* "Surely it was time someone invented a new plot."[26] Surely it was time for a new vision.

Virginia Woolf, distanced as she was by her sex and her experience, from the patriarchal thought of her contemporaries had a hypothetical solution to the problems of civilisation: she envisioned a world continually regenerated by the power of art and the power of language; a world remade from all that was worth keeping from the untidy remnants of the old, united with a new plot to which all living things contributed. Such a fusion of past and present might uncover the true meaning of life, if only in small epiphanies, moments of transcendence, "moments of being," which to prevent regression or stasis must be continually sought and renewed.

Woolf's vision of the unity of all things requires cooperation between the sexes. In *A Room of One's Own* she pondered the meaning of "unity of the mind" yet seemed to reject the convergence which is perhaps implied by androgyny.[27] If convergence is "a movement directed toward or terminating in the same point," it would result in stasis.[28] Woolf points out that Coleridge's definition of an androgynous mind may be an open or "porous" mind, continually expanding, never static.[29] The sexes must each be receptive to the other's "womanliness" or "manliness," leaving room for what feminist critic Josephine Donovan calls "transcending visions."

The problem for Woolf as artist was to find a way, through her fiction, to focus the emotions aroused in ordinary people by a life that was generally unsatisfactory and in need of improvement. According to Josephine Donovan, the "prophetic mode" of criticism (of society through literature) requires a writer to do more than simply reflect changes that are occurring in the world; a writer must instead encourage a view of reality which may disagree with established views yet is closer to truth and so promotes human liberation.[30] Virginia Woolf, prophet for the modern world, promotes, in *Between the Acts,* the unity of reason and emotion, deemed philosophically incompatible but necessary for freedom and, it seems, for survival.

Woolf's prophetic method in *Between the Acts* was threefold: she first created a fictional artist, Miss La Trobe, who had Coleridge's "porous mind" to absorb the emotions and the logic of modern civilization, and the language to give them shape and meaning for her audience and for us, the readers. The artist remains more or less anonymous for she is the voice of the collective consciousness. Second, because her vision encompassed all life, Woolf then set her artist in Pointz Hall, a miniature world suspended in time and yet reminiscent of the ancient theater of Dionysos in Athens.

The artist creates the drama and sets it in a certain place, but for it to be effective there must be an audience. So the third aspect of Woolf's method, in keeping with the feeling that the function of art and culture is to unite all classes of men and women, is to require the reader to trust "the effect of the book on his mind," suggesting a kind of participatory reading of the text, merging the "imagination and insight" of the reader with the writer's own.[31]

For the purpose of clarification, both of Woolf's methods and of my own necessarily stumbling progress in the wake of her mercurial brilliance, I have roughly divided the arguments of this text to approximate her much more subtle divisions of the *Between the Acts*. The first chapter discusses the influence on Woolf's work of Jane Ellen Harrison, the archeologist, and the main components of the drama of the novel and the play within the novel: the artist, the setting and the audience. Chapter 2 is a two-part discussion of the characters and the events in the first section of the novel. The first part leads up to the coming together of all the symbolic characters at the meal in the dining room. The second part is a discussion of the significance of characters and events during and following the meal. I have as far as possible throughout the text discussed each character separately, but because all are interconnected, even enmeshed, I have done some forward-and backtracking among characters and events. Chapter 3 is a discussion of the pageant, and chapter 4 deals with the time following the departure of the fictional audience from Pointz Hall. And an afterword rather than a conclusion seems to be in keeping with the open ending of *Between the Acts*.

1

Theatre, Author, Audience

All living bodies have turned to dust and the Eternal Matter has transformed them into stones, into water, into clouds, while their souls have all been merged into one. This common soul of the world is I—I. . . . The souls of Alexander the Great, of Caesar, of Shakespeare, of Napoleon, and of the basest leech are contained in me!

Chekhov, *The Seagull*

Before discussing the mythical setting of the novel, Pointz Hall, the complex personae of Miss La Trobe, and the function of the audience, it would be useful to consider the influence on Virginia Woolf of the work of Jane Ellen Harrison, the archeologist. Woolf refers to Harrison, an old friend, several times in diaries and letters, and in *A Room of One's Own* the importance of Harrison's work to Woolf seems clear. Woolf refers obliquely to Jane Harrison as she walks in October, in what she calls a spring twilight, in the gardens of the fictional Fernham, really Newnham College, Cambridge. Significantly, I think, the Dionysiac regeneration ceremonies celebrating the start of the agricultural year in Greece, about which Harrison made important discoveries, began in autumn. Amid a profusion of spring flowers (in October) Woolf sees on the terrace "a bent figure, formidable yet humble, with her great forehead and her shabby dress—could it be the famous scholar, could it be J——H———herself?"[1] Harrison had remained what Woolf called an "outsider," an independent thinker who exemplified her own dictum that "spiritual creation à deux is a happening so rare as to be negligible." Harrison's major works were in Woolf's library, but it is *Ancient Art and Ritual* (1918), a Christmas present to Woolf in 1923 and a beautifully lucid discussion of the connection between ritual and art, the nature of art and its effect on modern life, that will help us to understand the political ideas in *Between the Acts*.

Ancient Art and Ritual sets out to show that ritual makes the bridge between life and art. Ritual as Harrison describes it is an action imitating something practical in life, for example, hunting, fishing or ploughing. Art is not useful (Woolf has told us that words are not useful) for it re/presents the action, ploughing perhaps, yet the common people are merely spectators of the presentation, not participants as they are in the ritual dance designed to make the ploughed furrows fertile. So art, in this case the re/enactment of the re/action to a barren field, is an end in itself. One can, of course, connect Woolf's concern with the development of a common language, which I will discuss later, with the development of art from ritual.

The connection art has with life is over the ritual bridge, a bridge left behind when we no longer believe in the efficacy of certain rites; we get pleasure from their beauty or their drama but once the collective emotion, hunger or hate, for instance, which inspired the ritual rain dance or war dance has faded, the action loses importance in a world in which individual heroes have taken the place of gods.

One form of ritual participation was dancing by the common people, by "tillers of the earth, who danced when they rested from sowing and ploughing."[2] The familiar plot was the cycle of death and life or summer and winter, requiring only one actor and no attention from an audience, no looking, for all were dancers, all were participants. When stories of human, individual heroes were gradually added to the old, monotonous plot of seasonal death and rebirth, those not acting out the heroes' exploits became watchers, and in the case of language, critics and readers. The transition from ritual to art was not sudden and complete. Vestiges of ritual remain: propitiary rites for a god imagined at a time of great emotion, the giver of what may be desired and is unaccomplished.

The connection between the ancient ritual to propitiate the god and to satisfy the needs and desires of the people, and the art which is the drama is, Harrison tells us, not easy to track if we look only at the example of ancient Greece. The Greeks moved swiftly from ritual to art. On the other hand the Egyptians, although maintaining an advanced civilization for three thousand years, never developed their drama beyond the ritual stage. There is evidence to suggest that the god Dionysos may be another version of Osiris; this shifting perspective suited the primitive, preliterate mind as it suits Virginia Woolf whose "new plot" is more ancient than language itself. Jane Harrison warns us:

> It is only by a somewhat severe mental effort that we realize . . . there were no gods at all, . . . only conceptions of the human mind, shifting and changing colour with every human mind that conceived them. . . . [W]e should think back the "many" we have so sharply and strenuously divided, into the haze of the primitive "one."[3]

One is thankful to have this bit of advice, but at this point, if we isolate Dionysos and the Greeks from the primitive haze, we can begin to understand why Woolf adopted Harrison's work as a means of expressing her own political views in *Between the Acts.*

Peisistratos, a democratic tyrant in the sixth century B.C. is credited with responsibility for the change in Greek theatre from ritual to art. Tyranny is, in the Greek sense, benevolent and not, as in the modern sense, oppressive. The tyrant, raised to his position by the workers, stood as did Dionysos the god, for the people. His task was "to help and serve the common people" (AR 153). The descendants of Dionysos, the spirit of new birth in spring, the king and queen of the May, also come from the working classes. The aristocracy—conservative then as now—if they worshipped anything, worshipped their own ancestors, their own traditions, their own land. Peisistratos knew that the city, where democracy began, where wealth and land are acquired, not inherited, needed Dionysos the god of the people; he built a temple and orchestra or dancing place in Athens, extending the worship of the god to the city.

If we examine Jane Harrison's line drawing of the early Dionysiac theatre at Athens we can see clearly the wall of the precinct behind the the two temples: the first built in 530 B.C. by Peisistratos and the larger two hundred years later (AR 144). The orchestra or dancing circle is built against the south side of the Acropolis. The later temple is on the north side, the wall of the precinct apparently continuing the temple and facing the west, the high afternoon and the setting evening sun (AR 142–45).

Harrison describes the development of early Greek theatre after Peisistratos: the seating arrangements, the dressing room, and the rudimentary stage from which the prologue might be spoken or the play might be played out. The spectators who had once been participants—some dancers remained as the chorus—sat on wooden seats without backs in the open air theatre. The front row of seats was reserved for dignitaries, usually priests and state officials. At the centre, flanked by the priest of Apollo the laurel-bearer and the priest of Olympian Zeus, sat the priest of Dionysos. The day the drama was performed was always an occasion of high festivity; preparations in the consecrated place of worship, separate from the place of the ordinary citizens' everyday life and work, began at dawn and continued all day. Although the festival was dedicated to the god, the actors did not impersonate gods and goddesses but instead, on this day of religious worship, played out stories of Homeric heroes and heroines.

The stories played out at the village pageant in *Between the Acts* are unrecorded episodes of the history of England. Nonetheless the setting, both of the pageant and of the novel itself, Pointz Hall and its grounds, is Woolf's unorthodox recreation of Greek theatre as described by Harrison. The drama is Woolf's version of the worship of Dionysos, a version considerably adulterated with appropriations from cultures other than ancient Greece. The rudimentary theatre is reminiscent of Harrison's description of the Acropolis. The stone stage is the terrace outside Pointz Hall. The temple or stone house is the hall itself, built before the reformation in "the hollow facing North" (10). The barn built in the thirteenth century is, in Woolf's mythical world, the older temple built to honor Dionysos by the tyrant Peisistratos. The fact that the barn is older than the house emphasises for us that animals existed before humans.

The chorus of villagers, "tillers of the earth," dances and sings in the sacred circle of the dancing place, the orchestra behind the terrace, cut off from it by the tall trees. A soapbox is the "rude platform" from which the prologue is spoken, on which the symbolic figures of the three great ages of English history appear, and on which the Reverend G. W. Streatfield stands to sum up his impressions of the performance. The spectators, the ordinary citizens, pass the two symbolic timeless view from the house: "'It'll be there,' she nodded at the strip of gauze laid upon the distant fields, 'when we're not'" (43). Natural happenings, the as Woolf puts it, "they had a duty to society" (78). A wall extends from Pointz Hall "on the raised ground in the sun," and seems to correspond to the wall of the ancient precinct of the Acropolis (42).

Harrison points out that "the drama of man's life is acted out for us against a tremendous background of natural happenings: a background that preceded man and will outlast him" (AR 199). Lucy Swithin understands the significance of the timeless view from the house: " 'It'll be there,' she nodded at the strip of gauze laid upon the distant fields, 'when we're not' " (43). Natural happenings, the view, the weather, the behaviour of birds and animals, historic and prehistoric, affect the action as much as any character does, in the pageant and in the novel itself. The visual background to the lives of the inhabitants of Pointz Hall reveals little to them in the way of new ideas: "They looked at what they knew to see if what they knew might perhaps be different today. Most days it was the same" (43). Until Miss La Trobe poses her scenes and characters in front of the unchanging view in the heat, solid and unavoidable as in Greece or Egypt, little comes to mind but "senseless, hideous, stupefying" repetition—no new plots, no progress (53).

The quest for relief from the terrifying paralysis thus implied is the quest on which Woolf sets her characters and her readers in the setting, the space and time of the novel: all, in a sense are the same. The action of the novel is enclosed chronologically within one turn of the earth on its axis, spatially within the ground of Pointz Hall. Greek art has shown that the years "are not abstractions, divisions of time; they are the substance, the content of time. . . . "[4] The twenty-four hours at Pointz Hall are equally substantial in the same sense.

The name suggests that the house is central to the novel, that all the action radiates from it or turns upon it as on a pivot. In prepatriarchal mythology the omphalos or sacred conical stone at Delphi was considered the central point of the universe. A concept of the earth turning on its axis did not exist, but instead the year itself had a turning point, distinct from the entire revolution. At first a year was a lunar year, thirty days, and was itself a ring possible to visualise, or an invisible moment, a revolution. The omphalos, sacred to the mother goddess Gaia or Ge, the earliest possessor of the oracle, was then the central point on earth *and* the central point in time. A ring was concrete, visible, in the present; a revolution was abstract, past as soon as realised. So Pointz Hall is both concrete, a spatial centre, in the present, and a place in which we are reminded of the revolutions of chronological time past.

Jane Marcus argues that Virginia Woolf conceived of chronological or clock time as male and the antithesis of emotional life.[5] The intricate mechanism of a watch symbolizes the clear analytical thought of the Age of Enlightenment. Woolf must have known Jane Harrison's position that the modern habit of analytical thought is a barrier to realising mythology, so she smashes the ticking watch at the battle of Waterloo—by which time reason had in any case fallen to military power—and enshrines it under glass on the upstairs landing in Pointz Hall, as a curiosity left by a long-dead servant. She then invents her own symbol, the ticking machine in the bushes controlled by La Trobe, the artist, who is, as we shall see, the voice of reason *and* emotion (10).[6]

The setting of the novel then is on one level an English country house in June 1939; on another level it is the ancient Dionysiac theatre of Athens. Woolf's theatre is influenced, as was the original, by other mythologies and cultures closer to nature than we, actively worshipping gods and goddesses whose favors—sun, rain, birth—meant survival. In addition, and consistent with the vision of unity with which Woolf was ever preoccupied, is her population of the entire setting of the novel with phantoms of English history and literature, either personified or remembered, sometimes only dimly, by almost all of the characters. While the earth turns once, Woolf uses these ghosts, through comedic illusion, especially the temporary suspension of chronological time, to jerk both the reader and the fictional audience to and from the point where they stand, into "present time reality" (130). The effect on the audience and on the reader of the novel, once they understand the several levels of meaning, is to make them conscious, through dramatic devices, particularly the plays within the play, of their own alienation and to draw them into the collective emotion. La Trobe's "porous" mind—"every cell in her body was absorbent"—soaks up the emotion and distills it into her artistic creation (111).

Miss La Trobe is a formidable figure. In ancient civilisations the giver of all life was the mother goddess. Jane Marcus and others have suggested that La Trobe symbolises the very ancient, prepatriarchal mother-maid deity who presided over fertility rituals, sometimes in animal form.[7] La Trobe is mythic indeed. But she is also historic, contemporary, and metaphoric.

Art critic John Berger, in his essay "Why Look at Animals?" points to the magical as well as the useful function of animals for primitive peoples and suggests that the first metaphor may have been animal. He quotes Rousseau on the origins of language: "As emotions were the first motives which induced man to speak, his first utterances were tropes (metaphors). Figurative language was the first to be born; proper meanings were the last to be found."[8] Miss La Trobe is a living metaphor, a trope—or rather *the* trope—and the creator of emotion twice over (if her first persona is ancient matriarch). But she cannot be Woolf's anonymous voice unless emotion and reason are both present in a mode that can only be prophetic for it has never before attempted to encompass the whole of art and creation in a vision of a newly enlightened age. Emotion and nature appear in La Trobe as metaphor, and in La Trobe as goddess. Reason too is there, visible to those who understand the many-sided nature of words.

The Age of Reason or Enlightenment produced a figure who became known as the "intellectual master of Europe": Arouet le Jeune, or as he called himself, Voltaire. A picture of Voltaire in old age, wizened and monkey-faced, hung over the mantlepiece in the study of the country home of Virginia Woolf's friend Lytton Strachey. According to biographer Leon Edel, Strachey had always admired the scholar whose work, like Strachey's own, "challenged and mocked Church and State and the military."[9] Strachey, in fact, fancied himself in dreams to be a second Voltaire. Virginia Woolf may have felt better qualified than Strachey to succeed Voltaire, for in *Three Guineas* she too had proved to be a foe of church, state and military. Indeed Voltaire's cry, *"écrasez l'infâme"*—crush the infamous thing—is echoed in Woolf's "crush him in our own country."[10] And in December 1940 Lady Margot Oxford, a woman infatuated with Virginia Woolf, sent her as a tribute to her ferocious intellect a bronze statuette of Voltaire.[11]

Voltaire may have formed his literary name as an anagram of Arouet le J(eune). If so, the *U* and *J* became *V* and *I*. Possibly Virginia Woolf formed La Trobe as an anagram of Voltaire. She substituted *B* for *V* and eliminated *I*. When writing to her sister Vanessa, Woolf was accustomed to signing herself *B* (for Billy Goat). The goat, as Jane Harrison tells us, is a determined life spirit able to survive in dry and stony lands (T 206). Woolf wrote many times of her dislike of the letter *I,* its dominance and the "aridity, which it casts within its shade."[12] If she was to keep her own figure "fictitious; legendary," it was entirely appropriate that she remove the egotistical symbol *I* and her own identification, the initial *V*, from the name of the anonymous woman-man she created as the creator of the new visionary age of which she—Woolf—was the prophet. To give a little more weight to the argument, the nickname Woolf gave La Trobe may also have associations with the age of reason.

Between the Acts is in some sense an epic, giving voice as it does to the ideals of a civilised world. The eighteenth century was greatly influenced by a French cleric named Le Bossu, who published in 1675 a set of rules for the composition of epic poetry. He insisted that the primary focus of the epic was the moral lesson it conveyed. Voltaire's 1727 reply to Le Bossu was more concerned with the relationship of the epic to its culture than with its form, a progression leading eventually to the modern novel.[13] Woolf saw the need for experimentation with literary form, she understood the morality of collective behavior, and she had to show the way to heal the cracks in a fractured civilisation and to connect the old world with the new. So La Trobe's nickname among the villagers is Bossy—a common English name for a cow and for a "boss-eyed" person, one whose vision is oblique or slant. And, in dialect, a boss is the tray or hod used by a plasterer or bricklayer to carry bricks and mortar.[14]

If we accept this hypothesis, we can say that the brilliant, economical arrangement of letters makes the creative artist—the perverse, independent homosexual writer Miss La Trobe—a figure of multiple significance. At one time she is the ancient, horned cow goddess, primeval mother of all creation, part animal, part human; the intellectual genius of Europe, the foe of church, state and military; the obscure yet influential French cleric who ruled that the epic must convey a moral lesson; the creator of a new language; and an artisan as well as artist, equipped with the material to unite ill-fitting and disparate elements. In any event it is a useful construct that gives to La Trobe the dimensions she must have for her unique and lonely function as Harrison's "world soul" (AR 246). The lonely La Trobe seeks the hospitable shelter of the village inn among the common people; Voltaire was given the ironic title "Inn Keeper of Europe" for his hospitality to the literati and aristocracy at Ferney, the country estate where he wrote *Candide*. La Trobe's inspiration, like Lytton Strachey's, is a painting of her literary mentor: "a cow in a stable" (153). So Woolf emphasises the utterly subversive nature of the artist as she saw her and as she saw herself: an outsider, a lover of women, lonely and misunderstood. She knew also she was an artistic genius with the requisites for creation: detachment, a room of her own, determination in the face of criticism, and a slant view of the world both bleak and transcendent.

La Trobe, outwardly a humble figure, unattractive, overweight and badly dressed, is also like the ancient Peisistratos, a benevolent tyrant, a leader of the masses: "No one liked to be ordered about singly, but in little troops they appealed to her. Someone must lead" (50). The desire for change and for growth takes the form of a quest on which Woolf sets her characters and indirectly ourselves. The initiator and leader of the quest, essentially the quest of the knights of the grail, is La Trobe. The questing hero is not one man but the race, the common people seeking through language, new life, meaning to life and to death and an end to human pain. The collective journey is a spiritual voyage by water, seeking water—water symbolizing emotion and life—which as the second sentence of the novel indicates, will never be supplied by the capitalist institutions that control civilisation: "The county council had promised to bring water to the village but they hadn't" (7). The impetus for the voyage and the direction it takes depends on the artist: "Miss La Trobe had the look of a commander pacing his deck" (49). The collective hero, ourselves, will heal the wounds of the earth, not by the lance, as Wagner's Parsifal the "guileless fool" healed the wounds of Amfortas the suffering king, thereby ending his pain, but by *words* of mutual understanding among both sexes, all classes, all of creation.[15] If speech is not found to heal the ailing land, to continue the cycle of death and rebirth, to continue the race (Woolf said words must embrace to continue the race), there will be no end to human pain.

The collective hero must ask the meaning of the drama. Leonard Woolf could not understand "why *Between the Acts* starts all over again at the end."[16] To his credit he asked the right question, a question that brings me to Virginia Woolf's third essential requirement, in addition to the writer and written or spoken text: the part played by the audience or the reader in a creative work. In the "present time" scene of the pageant, La Trobe forces the spectators to understand, through their reluctant participation in the drama, a "fraction of her meaning" (112). Of course her creativity is only made possible by their participation, for they are her inspiration; she is their "slave" (153). Woolf makes her meaning accessible to the heroes whose prophet she is, who ask the right questions. She has made clear that we can only do that through our own participation in her work.

In Virginia Woolf's introduction to the 1925 Modern Library edition of *Mrs. Dalloway* she refused to explain the meaning of the novel, offering instead the opinion that critics must trust their own judgment as to the effect of the book on the mind. Even if the writer attempted to elucidate all the autobiographical connections in a novel, it would still be the reader's task, using "imagination and insight," to decide what, if anything, was relevant. Furthermore she insisted, despite contemporary critical judgment to the contrary, that there was no particular method or form to which she consciously adhered when writing.[17] Virginia Woolf's acceptance that the effect of her work on the reader's mind is a valid basis for criticism demands, as I have said, a participatory reading of the text, merging the "imagination and insight" of the reader with her own. The reading of the work becomes then a shared creative experience: an experience that is never static and that is constantly renewed as readers from different environments and periods of history, with varied perspectives, take up the text.

Feminist criticism begins with an understanding of women's lives and history. Woolf has said that "books are the flowers or fruit stuck here and there on a tree which has its roots deep down in the earth of our earliest life, of our first experiences."[18] My reading of *Between the Acts* stems, in part, from a cultural heritage, as an Englishwoman, in common with Virginia Woolf. My working-class roots reach down, with her middle-class ones, into a common earth. Some of my interpretations are the result of taking a leap of the imagination from one familiar stone to another in the cultural foundation of English life, a life whose ways I absorbed before the foundation was shaken by the Second World War. My sense of the novel, that it requires more than a detached analysis, fits in with Woolf's theme of ritual participation in the drama and the collective emotion that inspires it.

The reason *Between the Acts* "starts all over again at the end" is because the end is only the end of the first act. The first act of the drama that Virginia Woolf presents to us is all of life; the second act begins with the final words of the text: "Then the curtain rose. They spoke" (159). *Between the Acts*, without a beginning or an end is just that: an interval to reflect on what is past and what will come next; a time for the actors, ourselves, to prepare and to decide how to play the second act.

Not only does *Between the Acts* begin where it ends, but it implies a new beginning: "Alpha not Omega" (T 535). The shape of the text is circular as the old Greek year, having gathered into the circle all experience to seethe and simmer as La Trobe "seethes wandering bodies and floating voices in a cauldron, and makes rise up from its amorphous mass a recreated world" (112). Woolf's cauldron is a deliberate artistic mélange which resists separation into the categories of history, myth, literature and contemporary life. Literary detective work leads, through following the clues offered by any of Woolf's allusions, on a circular tour. Like Lucy Swithin's "circular tour of the imagination—one making," it comes back to a starting point still contained within the cauldron or circle (127).

Any analysis, by attempting to reduce contextual complexities, may defeat the purpose of the novel if that purpose is, as it seems to be, unification. However, Woolf's repeated use of triple imagery suggests for the sake of convention a tri/vision into the before-pageant, pageant and after-pageant sections of the novel. Knowing that the text will likely resist such arbitrary sectioning, we stand, to begin, beneath the unclimbable branches of the monkey puzzle tree, in "the maze of the moon," her clear, pale light focused on Pointz Hall (41).

2

Prologue

Indeed all [men] have Isis and know her and the Gods of her company. . . . And there are consecrated symbols, some obscure ones and others more plain, guiding the intelligence towards the mysteries of the gods, [though] not without risk.

Plutarch

Pointz Hall is a large house with many rooms, spacious grounds, a greenhouse, stables, a lily pond, a terrace, lawns, a graveled driveway: all peopled by thespian goddesses and ghosts, barely disguised by the parts they are, for the moment, acting. They are almost weightless, difficult to peg down, merging as they drift from one historical moment to another. The house, as I have suggested, is a repository for all experience from the primeval to the present, a place which because it exists now in concrete form continues to be part of history, which is by definition abstract. We know the house is white and grey as a stone (9); the barn in which the community meets to feast and to talk, and to recall, perhaps without ever having been to Greece, a Greek temple, is raised on four conical stones, each one similar to the ancient omphalos (23).

The myth of Gaia tells of an oracle, inspired by mephitic vapors rising from the earth and spoken by a woman while she sits on a tripod over a crevice (T 386). The discussion in the big room with the windows open to the garden is about the cesspool, the source we may be sure of mephitic vapours (7). The county council, the state, has not kept its promise to bring water, symbol of emotional life, to the village to flush away to the cesspool the human excrement that inspires the oracle.

The cesspool, thus emblem of an ancient culture and part of the technological age, is set among the crisscross scars left by the struggle between the invaders and pillagers of the land and the agricultural communities trying to survive. The crisscross furrows of the plough are visible from an aeroplane—a detached and distant view, an artist's view—to remind us that the earth cannot be free until nature covers the scarred land with new growth.

Woolf extends the crisscross metaphor to the moment when Lucy Swithin reads a crisscross letter from Scarborough—the name apt and deliberately used by Woolf—then slips it between the pages of her *Outline of History* to mark the end of the chapter. Moments later Lucy vacates the room, leaving Isa and Giles to speak the first words of the next chapter or the second act in front of the window, still open to the garden, 24 hours after the discussion about the cesspool (158).

It seems then that the villagers may have access to the words of the oracle, to the vision of the tranced prophet, but only if their attention can be caught, if they can be made to listen to the sounds of nature, in this case the garden noises coming through the windows of the big room: "A cow coughed; . . . a bird chuckled outside" (7). The cow who coughs politely—cows seldom cough—is associated, like La Trobe, with the mother goddess portrayed in Egyptian myth as Hathor the horned one. In Egyptian mythology the earth's water supply came from Nut, the female sky goddess (known as Rhea to the Greeks) who gave birth out of Chaos to Isis, who is in turn identified with Hathor.[1]

In ancient history and mythology, animal signs were used universally for charting the experience of the world; animals lent their name or character to a quality that was in its essence mysterious.[2] So the curved arch of the sky became the underbelly of a cow, a sky goddess who while sometimes represented as a woman with toes and fingers touching the earth, was imagined as a heavenly cow.[3] Although animal signs were used, only humans could make them into symbols: a capacity inseparable from the development of language and, we may assume, the art of the writer.

If the coughing cow is a symbolic goddess then the chuckling bird is an omen: birds to the Greeks were magic potencies. The laughing woodpecker, one of the most ancient and powerful, a rain bird in charge of the weather, who "yaffles in our copses today," Woolf juxtaposes with the cow associated with the moisture-giving moon (T 101). Later in the impossible chaos of the "present time" scene among the mirrors, she writes of the unwise young who "shiver into splinters the old vision." The bird and the cow are there, frantically offering to contribute to the work of creation if someone will pay attention to the sounds they make and, through the human capacity for symbolic thought, transform those sounds into an image, a metaphor, a new language: "what a yaffle—as they call the laughing bird that flits from tree to tree . . . the very cows joined in. Walloping, tail lashing" (133, 134). The woodpecker splinters trees but does not "smash to atoms what was whole" (133). Woolf seeks through a rebirth of language a way to unite and a way to progress without total destruction of the old forms.

The chatter from the natural world of the garden and the discussion about the cesspool are interrupted when Isa Oliver enters the room "like a swan swimming its way" (8). She is surprised to find people in the room and lights burning. Her uncommon name Is/a suggests surprise, a question and an opening for discussion.[4] Isa, her name also short for Isabella, the Latin form of Elizabeth, wears Juno's peacocks on her dressing gown, faded peacocks: Juno the Roman goddess of marriage may be losing her place to Venus the goddess of love. Woolf alludes here to Shakespeare's reference to Juno's swans in *As You Like It*. Classical tradition has it that Juno's birds are peacocks; Venus' are swans.[5] Venus' or Aphrodite's beauty is implicit in the second part of Isa's name. Her goddess persona is established even before she sits, like the priestess of Gaia on her tripod, swaying as though ready to disappear into the ether, "on her three-cornered chair" (8).

The air in the room is tense with emotion between Isa, the would-be poet struggling to express herself in verse, and Rupert Haines, the mysterious gentleman farmer to whom she is attracted without really knowing why. Haines's "ravaged face," his passionate silence, his grey clothes make him a death figure. He is a farmer, the reaper of the corn in the fields around his house.

Rupert Haines handed Isa a cup of tea at their first meeting and a tennis racquet at their second: "that was all" (8). The cup suggests fertilising moisture, but the racquet, full of holes, is an imperfect phallus without the power of the sword or the spear. Isa's romantic daydream of herself and Haines floating downstream as swans on two perfect but opposing rings of Byron's poetry quoted by her husband's father is flawed: Isa is the moon who "walks in beauty like the night." Her light will be dimmed, even extinguished if she is seduced by Haines: "So we'll go no more a roving by the light of the moon." She fails to hold on to her vision of perfection in life allied with a male death figure, albeit disguised as a swan, much as she fails to hang on to her poetic vision long enough to find a suitable rhyme. She is tied to her domestic life, her poetry confined in an account book; Haines is tangled in the dirty duckweed that only grows in still or stagnant waters (8).

Haines is Hades, brother of Zeus, sometimes indistinguishable from him, sometimes known as Zeus of the underworld. He is the husband of Nemesis and the swan lover of Leda who, like Aphrodite and Nemesis in Robert Graves's version of the myth, is the nymph of death-in-life.[6] Isa sways, dissatisfied and uncertain, on her goddess chair. Her dark pigtails, Jungian symbols of illicit, even dirty sexuality, and at the same time symbols of Isis, mother of nature, fall over her bolster-shaped body. The bolster, originally baluster, is part of an ionic column resembling in shape the blossom of the pomegranate. We find later that Isa's "neck is broad as a pillar," the primitive form of the goddess once worshipped in Ilium (79). An ionic foot is a measure of verse in Greek and Latin poetry.

Isa is a multiple goddess: she is Isis, Ishtar, Venus, and Nemesis. Her "little boy who wasn't well" typifies the dying and resurrecting god of many Eastern cults, usually his mother's lover, who personifies the vegetation of the entire earth.[7] Isa is Persephone who by eating pomegranate seeds unknowingly forced her sorrowing mother to agree to her confinement underground for four months of every year. She is a poet—Isis is known as the first muse. Her goddess's power is shadowed by men and by modern life; her power to make poetry is driven underground by modern language. Clearly the world is ailing. Yet hope exists if Isis the muse is the questioning and questing Isa. Virginia Woolf deliberately slants and sub/verts the definitive state of being "is," replaces it with the indefinite article "a" and implies, instead of fact, conclusion or even determinism, simply "a thousand possibilities."

Rupert Haines too, linguistically, is much more than Hades or Osiris. His name is taken from the Old English "hain" meaning a hedge for keeping cattle away from a cornfield. *Haine* is the French noun for hate. Rupert of the Rhine was the German Prince who fought Oliver Cromwell at the Battle of Naseby, immortalized in Lord Macaulay's poem, collected in *Palgrave's Golden Treasury* and read by Woolf as a girl. Rupert is the "furious German . . . with his clarions and his drums" who "never comes but to conquer or to fall."[8] Rupert Brooke, who is remembered romantically as the lost poetic voice of a generation of Englishmen, was buried in the shade of ilex trees on the isle of Skyros, also the burial place of Theseus; Brooke died on April 23, 1915, the day of Shakespeare and of Saint George.[9] In *Between the Acts* Isa gets her last look at Rupert Haines as he vanishes "in the crowd by the ilex" (73).

Virginia Woolf's ingenuity is unbounded: Haines is also the unimaginative Englishman encountered in the first section of James Joyce's *Ulysses* staying in a Martello tower, one of 74 such fortifications built in 1804 along the English and Irish coasts to repel a possible French sea attack, and named for the grandfather of Charlemagne and slaughterer of vast numbers of Saracens at Tours in the seventh century, Charles Martel (The Hammer).[10] Joyce's Haines is modeled after a man who terrified Joyce with a gun in a Martello tower which, it was predicted, would become the omphalos of a new Delphi situated in Ireland if Joyce remained there to write *Ulysses*. Joyce left Ireland almost immediately after the shooting incident.[11]

Woolf's use of Joyce's fictional name for the man who was symbolic to him of all the religious and social forces opposing him, as the name of her own fictional figure of death, shows a certain sympathy for and artistic and political alliance with Joyce. She recognized the importance of Joyce's work to liberate modern literature from nineteenth-century convention, but she wanted to go further. In *Between the Acts* a hammer becomes symbolic of male aggression toward women in Isa's apocalyptic vision of the girl screaming in the barracks room, lured to see a horse with a green tail, the pale green horse of death. When Lucy Swithin comes in carrying Bart's hammer with which she nailed her announcement to the door of the barn, Isa's vision of rape shifts to one of resistance: "The girl screamed and hit him about the face with a hammer" (19, 20). And, typically in Woolf's transformational symbolism, the hammer takes on other, more positive significance in the hands of Lucy Swithin, as I will show later.

Woolf has, again in the name of a single character, this time antithetical to La Trobe yet connected to her by the invisible thread of mutual consciousness of the origins of the confines of language, personified all the institutions Woolf ridiculed in *Three Guineas* and La Trobe opposes in the village pageant in *Between the Acts:* church, state and military. The god of the underworld, the archpatriarch of Olympus, the hated German fascist from across the channel, the middle-class Englishman, and the purveyor of the language of oppression, the male writer, represent all the forces Woolf fears may destroy civilization by refusing to invent a "new plot." In addition she arbitrarily lifts Joyce's new Delphi and "navel stone" out of Ireland, together with the Celtic Magna Dea, and deposits them where she obviously feels they will be in safer hands, at Pointz Hall.

So on the mythical level, if Isa is the horned cow goddess, she cannot associate with Haines without compromising or losing her powerful divinity and trampling on the corn growing around his house. On the practical and artistic level she must remain, as Woolf herself and Miss La Trobe remain, an outsider: a member of the society proposed in *Three Guineas* which will cooperate with men but never be coopted by them. The glimmer of hope which shows in Woolf's portrait of Haines and which supports the idea of connection, however tenuous, with James Joyce and other writers, comes from the cornfield. Hades has some associations with the fertility of the earth; he is a grim figure in mythology but not really a malignant one.

His mysterious presence influences the conversation on the terrace after lunch. Inarticulate Giles has no words to express his anger at the coming war. Mrs. Manresa, determinedly optimistic and apparently loving life, certainly flirting with Bart, Giles and even Candish the butler, speaks the first words of Hamlet's soliloquy to death. Unhappy Isa quotes and misquotes with William Dodge part of the third stanza of Keats's "Ode to a Nightingale," in which the poet is "half in love with easeful death." Lucy Swithin knows that the words of poets are not the common voice today. Emotion in 1939 is "hidden behind the eyes," difficult to convey with words. Mrs. Manresa passes on "sensations" or emotions without a word to Giles and to Bartholomew who puzzles over the mystery of "thoughts without words" (44).

The ancients kept in touch with their gods through sacrifice, originally a means of communication rather than of gain for the gods and loss for humanity. Eating your totem, in this case filet of fish, symbolic of goddesses and of life from immemorial time, establishes a thread like Mrs. Manresa's thread of sensation uniting the luncheon party at Pointz Hall before the pageant (T 138). The problem La Trobe addresses in the pageant is to find a means by which death may be part of the process of life toward immortality through regeneration, rather than a systematic destruction of all life with no hope for renewal. Woolf's solution is to find a common language, the thread of which will unite past, present, future, death and life and which death, inevitable in life, will not destroy.

Acacia blossoms drift over Haines's car in Isa's final imaginative vision of him. The red and white blooms of the evergreen are symbols for immortality beyond death. Immortality implies regeneration; humans must pass first through the grave by the due enactment of death-in-life, common to all and personified in mythology by the nymph goddesses Aphrodite, and Nemesis in a form worshipped earlier than the goddess of individual vengeance she came to be as Hades' wife.[12] Jane Harrison points out "It is when the old tribal sanctions are broken down that Aidos and Nemesis of and for the individual come into force" (T 29). In the drawing room at Pointz Hall the goose-faced Mrs. Haines promises to destroy the feeling between Isa and Haines "as the thrush pecks the wings off a butterfly" (9). She is vengeful indeed. Yet when she rises to leave she expects Isa to rise at the same time, for they were both in another time and place goddesses of the moon, bound to rise in unison, tied by a common mythical past.

Nemesis took the form of a goose to escape the attention of Zeus, the swan god who raped her. The daughter of Night, the mother goddess Nyx, vaguely remembers her earlier mythic origins and the flight of the sacred swans far north to unknown breeding grounds where chuckling birds or nightingales do not venture (7).[13] Of course she is not afraid of cows. She fears the powerful cart horse, an equine male reminding her perhaps of Zeus' and Hades' brother Poseidon. Mrs. Haines is Nemesis for the individual; centuries of family graves in the churchyard, her credentials for ancestor worship, set her apart from Bart Oliver whose family has been at Pointz Hall only since Wellington defeated Napoleon, little more than 120 years ago.[14]

Old Bart Oliver remembers his mother; "she was very stout; kept her tea caddy locked; yet had given him . . . a copy of Byron" (8). In prepatriarchal myth, before Hesiod reshaped the myth, as Jane Harrison tells us, "to his own bourgeois pessimistic ends," Pandora was earth mother and "giver of all gifts." Her figure like Bart's mother's was full and round as the vase which contained her gifts. Harrison discusses the representation in early Greek art of Pandora rising head first from the earth to meet the blows of the hammers which were the primitive tools used by men for breaking clods of earth before the existence of the spade.[15] So Bart recalls a time of great antiquity, the role of his mother the earth, and an early positive significance of the hammer now in his possession and so greatly distorted by men as an instrument of aggression. The gift he remembers is his mother's gift of poetry, the poetry which, despite his age, he can still recite.

Old Bart Oliver is more than old. He is close to death. We read of his "veins swollen . . . with a brownish fluid" as though he is embalmed or mummified. This connects him with the dead Osiris, found grown into the trunk of a tree by Isis, his wife, mother and sister, and by Anubis, Isis' dog and child and later a god of the dead and of embalmers.[16] Bart seems to love his son Giles and his dog Sohrab, his "familiar spirit," with equal devotion (87).

Matthew Arnold's tragic poem "Sohrab and Rustum" tells of a Persian warrior Rustum who unknowingly wounds with a spear his own son, the hero of the Tartars, believing his child is a "slight, helpless girl." Too late, Rustum recognizes him by his seal, the signet branded into Sohrab's arm by his mother.

Sohrab dies after he "took the spear and drew it from his side, . . . / and life / Flowed with the stream." In Arnold's poem Rustum the warrior mourns, seated beside the body of his dead child, on the cold sands of the desert.[17]

In *Between the Acts* Sohrab the Afghan hound guards his master like a "crusader's dog . . . even in the realms of death" (17). Bart's dream of India becomes a dream, perhaps of Persia or a desert battlefield in a crusading war against the infidels, a male-created scene of the aridity of death. Later Bart is unable to find words to express his feeling that, like the chorus of old men in Aristophanes's *Lysistrata,* he is left "with no glow on the log." Mrs. Manresa "ripped the rag doll and let the sawdust stream from his heart," the heart of T. S. Eliot's "stuffed men" and an echo of Arnold's "life / Flowed with the stream" (147).[18]

Giles wears a signet ring not on his arm but on his little finger (48); Miss La Trobe's appearance is vaguely reminiscent of a Tartar, a Russian.[19] She is not "altogether a lady" (46). She strides the countryside, carrying her castigating whip. Although she is the stereotype of a lesbian woman, and a tartar in the colloquial sense of being intractable, she is also Woolf's answer to Matthew Arnold's glorification of the silly heroics of Sohrab the Tartar warrior who wanted a fight to the death so that his fame would reach the ears of his father Rustum; who only made his father *see,* that is know him as his son, after Rustum had mortally wounded him. In Arnold's poem, Sohrab and Rustum both ignore their intuition, their emotion, in favor of the reason and logic that lead to filicide and an anagnorisis which cannot be followed by epiphany, for in the waterless desert there is nothing from which new life can arise.

La Trobe is the antithesis of Arnold's "slight, helpless girl, . . . / made pale by words."[20] Far from making La Trobe pale, words come to life within her; she uses "strong language" (16). She must make her audience *see* by the power of language, which has taken root and grown in the broth, the fertile medium which is her mind. So Virginia Woolf's alternative for women forced to be silent and to sacrifice the life they have created within them, and for men who refuse to question the value of honor, patriotism and the rule of law is the "new plot," continually recreated by the artist, the anonymous voice which comes in part from the ancient world.

Bart epitomises law and reason; a repository of facts, he alone knows how distant is the sea "as if he had whipped a tape measure from his pocket and measured it exactly" (25, 26). He would "carry the torch of reason till it went out in the darkness of the cave" (149). Bart can only be comfortable if he confines his vision in a frame. He surveys the world from his prison of reason and logic, a noose always with him: "Had he been a painter, he would have fixed his easel . . . where the country, barred by trees, looked like a picture" (14).

Bart, a homonym of barred and a shortened form of the title "baronet" given to commoner landowners, is also a diminutive of Bartholomew, one of Christ's twelve apostles. (Leonard Woolf and many of Virginia Woolf's male friends belonged to the society of intellectuals, the Apostles, at Cambridge.) According to tradition, Bartholomew was a fisherman who preached the gospel in India and eventually was flayed alive.[21] An oliver is a tilt hammer, powered by a spring and sometimes used for making nails. Oliver is also the olive tree, holy to the Greeks and sacred to Athena and the moon goddess (T 191).

So Bart, his land acquired only 120 years ago, retired from the Indian civil service, keeps his fishing tackle, no longer used, tidily in a cupboard with his hammer and nails. His old man's skin is thin and loose; it shudders "as a dog shudders its skin" or as though the skin has been separated from the flesh or flayed (158). A man of reason and high intellect, Bart finds it increasingly difficult, as he grows old, to nail down facts and to build civilised structures with his hammer. Dimly, he is conscious of an earlier use of the hammer to set free rather than to confine, so he keeps it at hand, with his fishing line, his "thread of life." He is also a moon man and reminiscent of the ancient Eastern animal gods which emerged long ago from the "primitive haze."

One other association comes from the sound of Bart Oliver: a sound not unlike Bath Oliver, a flat, dry English biscuit invented in the sixteenth century. The biscuit is easily crumbled, and Woolf refers to it in her diary.[22] Crumb is one of Woolf's metaphors for tedious words imparting dry facts, negating imagination, discouraging initiative and creativity and presented as receivable truth.

The crumbs or words of the dry Bart (or Bath) Oliver have been acquired initially from the volumes of male-inspired writing lining the library shelves at Pointz Hall. (The tortoise-shell butterfly—female creative power—beats impatiently but persistently outside on the window pane.) Bart Oliver is a literary man. La Trobe and Voltaire are contained within the letters of his name. His mind has reaped not corn but a great harvest of knowledge from his gentleman's library of gentlemen's books by gentlemen writers, all of whom may be included among the men symbolically represented by Rupert Haines: poets Keats, Shelley, Yeats and Donne, the meaning of death their major preoccupation; statesmen and soldiers Garibaldi, Wellington and Palmerston; scientists Darwin, Eddington, Jeans; the authors of reports on horses and irrigation (implying a need for moisture) and histories of the old cities Durham and Nottingham.

Bart reads the daily paper to shore up his supply of facts. He is an old man and weary. His life will continue through his son whom he loves, and through Isa toward whom he feels gratitude for "stretching his thread of life so fine, so far" (17). She who "in her striped dress continued him" wears the many-colored veil or robe of Isis representing the diversity of nature. All life is clothed in Isis' mantle.[23] So Bart takes his last snap at the paper like a dog snapping at a biscuit, before handing it, the symbol of his knowledge, on to Giles in the last scene: "'Finished?' said Giles taking it from his father. The old man relinquished his paper" (157).

Bart's grandchildren take their morning outing around the garden with their nurses Mabel and Amy, both named for Mater Amabilis, a title of the Virgin mother of Christ. The baby Caro—perhaps a mythical Core or Kore or future Carline wife, one of Demeter's names—is rolled by her guardians in the perambulator. Artemis in her ancient form as great mother held a festival of nurses and nurslings and as virgin priestess is said to have traveled in a car drawn by deer (T 504, 505). The baby throws her furry bear, Artemis' symbol as bear goddess, onto the grass. The nurses gather up the bear, for it is their totem, their protector, and the baby girl must be taught reverence for animals if she is to be part of the reborn world (T 450).

Little George walks slowly behind (he is only partially recovered from his illness). Too young to read, he listens often to the banal, uneducated language of the nurses. His moment of pure rapture, a vision of the unity, harmony and balance of all things as he gathers, like Persephone, the soft yellow flower, is shattered by his grandfather's appearance as a "terrible peaked, eyeless monster," the ubiquitous newspaper rolled into a "beak," always Virginia Woolf's metaphor for masculine insensitivity (13).[24] Bart is wearing his Hades costume: his ancestral home, facing away from the sun, once boasted four horses to drag the family coach through the mud (10); his invocations are to Jupiter and to Zeus the maker of thunder; he also appears to George as the dragon he has to slay (20, 28).

The Afghan hound with long nose and wild yellow eyes, Bart's dog from the far country of the East, accompanying his master on his morning walk, conjures up images of Anubis and of Thoth the Egyptian, dog-faced god of speech, intelligence, law and order, the inventor of letters and of writing. Thoth was sometimes revered as the sacred Ibis, a bird with an extraordinarily long, curved beak. The "fleck of foam" always on the dog's nostril suggests new birth and the male seed: Aphrodite was foam born, supposedly from the severed genitals of Uranus the sky god (87, 148).[25] Woolf's imagery of male power and dominance, extending to aridity and death is constantly challenged by small persistent signs of life: the newspaper beak or snout—ibis or dog, male-invented intelligence, logic and speech—encounters the pure emotional tears of a child; the seed of life, awaiting only love, clings to the nostril of the god (dog), ready to in/spire and to become a cooperative creation, perhaps a new language.

To Woolf, Bart is the "old vision" still with some merit—Giles only crumples the newspaper, does not destroy it—while George, unsullied by middle-class, educated, masculine-inspired language can have an epiphany, can avoid the old man's noose, can still shed tears of life and feeling. "'Your little boy's a cry-baby,' " is a sign to Isa—Venus, protector of her son and Isis, destroyer as well as healer—that the old man's beard, the bitter herb which grows outside the nursery window must be stripped away before it chokes off roses *and words:* "In passing she stripped the bitter leaf that grew, as it happened, outside the nursery window. Old Man's Beard. Shrivelling the shreds in lieu of words, for no words grow there, nor roses either, she swept past . . . 'like Venus . . . to her prey . . . ' " (151). Isa is determined that her little boy will learn a language grown side-by-side with roses, the symbol of pure love, and that, like Antigone, he will join in loving not in hating.[26] The thread of life joining Bart to his grandson is his only route to immortality, so the little boy must not become fatally infected with the ills of bearded men.

Indeed Woolf's response to the assumed prerogative of the conventionally educated classes to be writers was to use the metaphor of the back stairs as a suggested route by which the uneducated could invade the ivory towers or the upper stories of the house of language.[27] Pointz Hall has a principal staircase leading to the landing on which the books of poets "from whom we descend by way of the mind" are kept (54). Another, "a mere ladder at the back," is intended for the servants to ascend to the bedrooms where life is conceived (9). So the words of Keats, Donne and even Wellington may embrace the unvarnished speech of peasants and servants in Woolf's sexual metaphor for the exogamous production of new and vigorous life and language.

Reason and emotion, the male and female principles, mingle as in a "mist" in Bart and his sister Lucy Swithin. Lucy is accustomed to her brother's superior attitude when he is discomfited and feels unable to control a world unbounded; his symbolic significance, linguistically and metaphorically, is closely connected to his sister and complemented by her qualities and the many roles she plays in the drama. So far I have only mentioned Lucy's significance as Bart's symbolic sister/wife and as Ishtar, another very ancient form of Aphrodite. Lucy has, in addition to her close connection with Bart, a clinging, persistent quality causing her to lie lightly, imperceptibly as gossamer, over the lives of all the characters: gentry, commoners and servants. She is elusive and swift as a bird or a fish darting, yet she is crucial to Woolf's purpose: creating a united but ever-changing world where all are free to play their "unacted part[s]" without fear.

Lucy has particular significance in relation to Isa as Isis, her symbolic inheritor, but it is impossible for any of the characters to ignore her as she speaks, muses, drifts and moves here and there in the time leading up to the assembly of the populace which she, by nailing up the placards, has called. Swithen or swither, in dialect, is to hesitate or to move swiftly but uncertainly from place to place. So, while discussing Lucy's importance in the novel I too must, where necessary, move and diverge, as she does, to touch on her connection with others.

Lucy, like Bart, is old and weary. Their " 'game's over' " (74). Lucy, three years younger than her brother, recalls a childhood like Maggie Tulliver's in George Eliot's *The Mill on the Floss,* sometimes fishing with her brother and gathering wildflowers in the meadows (20). Like Maggie she is subjected to fraternal teasing about her love for reading, but she bears the name of the cousin who went with Maggie and Tom on their walks and who was, in one sense, Maggie's antithesis and her rival. I have discussed the interchangeable nature of primitive deities. In addition divine pairs are often male and female aspects of the same goddess or god, and often the alliances are incestuous.[28] Bart as Tom Tulliver can love Lucy as Maggie for she is also Lucy Deane.

Among Lucy's several nicknames is her childhood name Cindy or *Sin*dy: "it could be spelt either way" (19). Cindy refers indirectly to Cinderella or cinders, a burnt substance retaining carbon and capable of further combustion; and swithen, in addition to moving swiftly, can mean to singe or scorch, to burn superficially or to cauterise: a healing process again connecting Lucy with Ishtar. The second spelling connects Lucy with Sinn the androgynous moon god of Babylon who was replaced by Ishtar. Bart is the male side of Sinn. Similarly in Egypt Osiris was superceded by Isis-Net, part male, part female.[29] Isa too is curiously bisexual in Woolf's description: "'Abortive,' was the word that expressed her." Her development sexually and artistically is somehow arrested at a rudimentary stage: "she never looked like Sappho, or one of the beautiful young men whose photographs adorned the weekly papers." Yet she is "Sir Richard's daughter," descended from the "Kings of Ireland"; socially she is acceptable, but her poetry is not worth writing down (16). When Bart shows his upper row of false teeth and Lucy remarks that "'marriages between cousins . . . can't be good for the teeth'" they are thinking of the incest permitted, even desired by a totemistic people, expecting renewal through reincarnation (26, T 271).

Woolf's comic preoccupation with teeth in *Between the Acts* results I suspect from her own lifelong dental problems. Bart's discussion with Lucy and Isa of the hazards of endogamy when applied to teeth is part of an elaborate metaphor for reincarnation for which teeth, those enduring bodily parts "gleaming like white seed corn," are the vehicles and symbolically significant (T 272). Bart's teeth are false. Isa visits her dentist regularly; her toothbrushes are prominent on the washstand where she prepares for her role as loving mother and wife. Her metaphorical toothache rages, unsatisfied by Bart's literature. In the rapidly changing world of 1939 in the seventh summer of the pageant the newspaper records only violence, and contains no words of love and renewal. Isa's toothache suggests a long and difficult rebirth. Her son is ailing but not dying. She is trying to give birth to a new language, an attempt which may end in the frustration of miscarriage or stillbirth.

Common people, the nurses are, of course, in danger of tooth decay from the sweets they suck; their words are thin transparencies, not solid information or ideas. Isa's dentist Bates—meaning the diminishing or waning moon—tells her false teeth were invented in the time of the Pharaohs, among whom brother and sister marriages were common.[30] Batty, Bates's partner—lunatic, affected with moon madness, perhaps a night creature, a bat—spends time repairing the decaying teeth of a princess. Lucy's comment before and after the discussion with Isa and Bart, that fish is hard to keep fresh, far away from the waters of the sea and rivers, is another reference to the desperate struggle to continue life that she, Isa, the girl in the barrack room, the nurses, the princess are waging without much help from inarticulate men like Giles, who "has no command of metaphor" and whose response to the anger he feels is to change his clothes and keep silent (43).

" 'That's the problem' " says Lucy Swithin with the superior wisdom of age and of women (25). Bart's sister, but much more than his sister, his alter ego—"what she saw he didn't and so on, *ad infinitum*"—is, as I have suggested, the apostle of unity in the novel (23). Although apparently an ineffectual old lady of little influence, she provides continuity, having difficulty, as many old ladies do, in separating the present from the past and in separating human beings from other creatures. "She belonged to the unifiers, [Bart] to the separatists" (88). Time, space, history and fiction combine and blur in Lucy Swithin, giving complexity to her relationships with other characters and multiple significance to her own.

She loses her place in her favorite book, *The Outline of History,* because history for her has no outline. It has no definable boundaries of time or space as she has none herself: The Victorians were no different from modern people, " 'only dressed differently' " (127). Unlike Bart she has no need for the security of a frame to protect her vision, for it is all embracing. She has only to kneel each night in communion with the Christian god who is also human, and to open her window to Dionysos who is one with humanity and with plants, birds, reptiles, all of nature. Lucy has an affinity with Lucina, goddess of childbirth, another version of Juno, connecting her with Isa and her dangerous confinement from which words may be reborn or may miscarry on the wind. As I have said she is Ishtar, one with Sinn (and Bart) and the predecessor of Isis (and Isa) as moon goddess, having many of her qualities. She trims sandwiches "triangular" (29); the servants call her "Batty" like Isa's dentist, or "Old Flimsy," for she too wears the veil of Isis hiding the true and the real beneath everyday worldly concerns. Lucy wears pearls; like the moon she is "the pearl in night's black ear," and she likes the portrait on the stairs "best in the moonlight" (11, 29, 54, 70).

Isa and Lucy are young and old visionaries, the fertile waxing moon and the waning, dark moon, still gleaming—Lucy's black shawl sparkles with sequins. Both are healers—Isa as Isis heals her child; Lucy as Ishtar heals William Dodge (155). Lucy's virginity distinguishes her from Isa. The ancient meaning of virgin is one who is not married rather than one who is chaste.[31] In this sense a widow or prostitute can be virgin. Lucy leans from the window of the upstairs passage where she has taken William Dodge, like Ishtar the virgin prostitute accepting and giving love freely, "she who peers out":[32] "And then a breeze blew and all the muslin blinds fluttered out, as if some majestic goddess, rising from her throne among her peers, had tossed her amber coloured raiment" (56, 57). The gravel below lies crescent or moon-shaped round the door; three white pigeons, Ishtar's symbol, rise from the grass and flutter away (54). Lucy's Christian cross when "pendant from her chain" visually becomes the *Crux Ansata,* sign of eternal life, sign of Venus, Aphrodite and Isis, as well as the familiar contemporary sign for woman. The sun, Apollo, brother of Artemis and originally an Eastern deity, a healer and lover of young men, strikes the golden cross. Dodge seems only to recognize the Christian significance. Yet he who is "half man," and aesthete rather than artist, is made whole through the compassion arising from Lucy's unselfish, virginal love (57). (I will elaborate later on Dodge's significance in Woolf's artistic and literary world).

Lucy's symbol as Ishtar is the dove or pigeon, but Lucy is bird herself. Ready to fly, she "perched on the edge of a chair like a bird on a telegraph wire" (87). She also wears "knobbed shoes as if she had claws corned like a canary's" (24). Bart misquotes the opening lines of Swinburne's poem, " 'O sister swallow, O sister swallow: / How can thy heart be full of the spring?' " (86) Swinburne's version of the myth of Procne and her sister Philomela is the lament of the nightingale Philomela for the swallow Procne who will "fly after spring to the south," the scene of the murder of her child, served to her husband Tereus as food in revenge for the rape and the silencing (by cutting out her tongue) of her sister.[33]

Bart's reprise of Philomela's lament for the sorrows of the "sister-swallow" who killed her child is given greater depth as we realize he is lamenting the loss of his own son. Lucy as swallow has no speech; Procne spoke to her sister "not in any language known to men" by weaving her story into a tapestry—a woman's art, literally a network, a crisscross both intricate and subversive. Bart cannot find his son; his library of works by men means "not . . . one damn" to him without Giles his inheritor and the extension of himself. Lucy, "an airball," cannot weight Giles as Bart would like him weighted: feet on the ground, pegged, framed and controllable. Then hope and reassurance, though no certainty, come from the garden, the natural world. Music and the dog-faced god of speech unite the speechless and the vocal briefly in a dance and a love song: imperfect and set in a minor key but for a time lessening Bart's despair (87, 88).

Bart is sceptical of the possibilities of peace and love. Lucy has the faith he lacks. She reads her *Outline of History* from 3:00 to 5:00 in the morning. Each year in winter, after dithering for a while, she retires to Hastings, vaguely resembling in her behavior the swallow and the death-in-life of T. S. Eliot's vision in *The Waste Land* of one who reads much of the night and goes south in the winter.[34] Lucy may inhabit one of the Martello towers that survive as private residences along the southeast coast near Hastings. But Lucy uses her hammer to announce a peaceful assembly rather than to deal a blow. The hammer which in Isa's mind becomes the instrument with which the girl assaulted by the troopers defends herself, symbolises the defence of women against the blows dealt them by men. And the assembly to which Lucy persistently (for seven summers) calls the populace is the pageant by which the artist can reveal her ever-changing vision. Woolf transforms the hammer in Lucy's hands from an instrument of death to one of life constantly renewed.

The village idiot "who always tore down what had been nailed up" crouches in the shade of the hedge, in the shadow of death, and laughs, as do the workers in the barn, at Lucy's words (24). Isa who admires Lucy's courage, for she too in old age is shadowed by death, describes her as "an angel" (21). Rather she is Saint Lucy, a Sicilian virgin martyr of the first century A.D., invoked against afflictions of the sight. Lucy kneels to protect her vision from the sword which executed her namesake. Fairly obviously she has connections with Saint Swithin, the bishop of Winchester who in 1093, shortly after the Norman invasion at Hastings, founded the cathedral and promised to send rain for forty consecutive days and nights if rain fell on his grave, on his feast day.[35]

Virginia Woolf sees Winchester as a place of male supremacy and death. At the school attended by generations of upper-class Englishmen one inhabits the world of the past, the world of the dead.[36] Not surprisingly La Trobe's teashop at Winchester "failed" (46). Lucy Swithin is an imaginary and considerably more lively, relative of Saint Swithin, the dead Catholic bishop whose offering of life like that of his church has certain conditions attached. Woolf weaves an imaginary history of Swithin's relative into *Between the Acts* much as she wove the story of Judith Shakespeare into *A Room of One's Own*.[37]

In primitive societies the making of rain and the control of the weather are usually in the hands of women.[38] A man (like Saint Swithin) is a rain maker only by virtue of his relation to a woman who holds the *real magic power,* the power of giving life. Lucy's birdlike magic is akin to the rain bird's, the laughing woodpecker's.

To the early Greeks, birds had the special magical power of actually making the weather. Long before Zeus hurled his thunderbolts the woodpecker, not a god but a sanctity, was held responsible for rain and for sunshine. By wearing feather robes or headdresses one could take to oneself some of the powers of the bird magician. Indeed, if one were of a totemistic people one became the bird. Isa's imaginative flight through the air, " 'there to lose what binds us here,' " depends on the "blue feather" from the bluebird-feather robe worn by Isis-Nephthys (15, 16, T 110). The words of Rupert Haines vibrate in Isa's consciousness like the propeller of an aeroplane, an ambiguous symbol and instrument of death and of freedom. She in turn cannot find a word to describe his effect on her and resists the temptation to follow him in imagination in favour of ordering fish for lunch. In the legend of Isis and Osiris, the goddess turns into a swallow to search for Osiris' body. So both Lucy and Isa participate in magic, through their mythical and imagined flights of the mind: Isa like Virginia Woolf herself in pursuit of elusive language, "shivering fragments"; Lucy gathering the connecting threads of the universe.[39]

Lucy's obsession with unity is not difficult to understand if we consider the influence of Jane Harrison's thought on Woolf's portrayal of this character. The "prayable being" whose existence in Lucy's skull puzzles Bart is Themis, daughter of Gaia and the personification of the religious principle itself (T 487). Harrison distinguishes religion, intellectualised and crystalized into an individual god external to humanity, and despised by Bart the rational thinker, from the representation of the collective conscience and social custom which is primitive religion: "Religion sums up and embodies what we feel together, what we care for together, what we imagine together" (T 487). Themis and Gaia are mother and daughter, "one in nature, many-named" (T 480).

Themis is earth mother, prophet of Delphi, and at the same time above and below every god and goddess, giving them the supporting structure of the social imperative (T 485). She has a prophetic function in the sense of utterance rather than of forecast; more than anything it is she who brings the gods together, "convenes and dissolves the assembly . . . presides over the feast" (T 482). She does not rule. She is no autocrat and never became a fully fledged divinity for she is part of them all. She represents the feeling of the group; she ranges from earth to heaven. Her allegiance is to none and her concern is for the law and justice common to all. She is doom or fate in the sense of the inevitability of the law she utters, the law arisen from primitive matrilineal society in which woman as mother was central.

Virginia Woolf's pacifism, her passionate belief that woman's nature is akin to Antigone's, is expressed by Jane Harrison in her justification of Themis as the "supreme social fact" whose dominance does not come from force because society is only possible "by co-operation, by mutual concession, not by antagonism" (T 492). Lucy Swithin as Themis is easy to trace. We know that she communes with Dionysos and with Christ. Harrison tells us "the essence of the Bacchic as contrasted with the Olympian religion is the doctrine of union and communion with the god" (T 48). Lucy is the spirit who reunites the sharply divided conceptions that are gods and blends them again into the universal and "primitive haze" from which they emerged.

Lucy cuts bread in the kitchen, close to the "semi-ecclesiastical" larder, and connects in her musings the theologies of several cultures. The dry Mrs. Sands loves cats, gods of ancient Egypt. The house cat's Chinese name Sun Yeng is changed in the kitchen to Sunny, an irreverent version of Apollo. Sands's predecessor was Jessie Pook, a primitive Puck or air spirit of times past, who was connected with Dionysos and who dropped hairpins into the soup. Zeus who solidified the sound of thunder into weapons inspired Bart's favorite oath but requires a more appropriate sacrifice than a hairpin. Lucy then skips, in thought, "sidelong, from yeast to alcohol; so to fermentation; so to Bacchus; and [lies] under purple lamps in a vineyard in Italy, as she had done often" (20).

Lucy is thus "in ecstasy and sacramental communion one with Bacchos" as she calls on others to become (T 487). She announces the assembly (the pageant), by nailing advance notices to the barn door. It is incumbent on her as Themis to make a society in which everyone has a place under the law. Because religion is what we feel, care for and imagine, it may exclude rational man. But the world has changed, as Bart reminds her: "what he saw she didn't . . . *ad infinitum*." Prayer is not enough for the modern world; she must "provide umbrellas" large enough for all to shelter beneath in order to ensure cooperation rather than antagonism (21).

Jane Harrison points out there were many themistes out of which arose the unifying spirit of Themis (T 483). And, most important, the unit of modern civilisation which, in Virginia Woolf's case is represented by the Victorian home and family which she satirises in the pageant, is not Themis but themis, for its internal law administered by paternal authority does not come under the umbrella of the collective conscience, that of the "herd instinct" (the bovine reference is significant) which *is* religion and which Mrs. Swithin indirectly personifies as the "old party with the umbrella right under the 'orse's nose," (a male horse), who defies the "laws of God and man" enforced by the phallic truncheon of Budge the Victorian policeman (118, T 485).

Themis "ranges all over" earth, sea and sky (T 483). Lightweight Lucy is forever poised for takeoff. She moves in her old garden shoes as if the earth were fluid. She mounts the stairs looking for someone praying in the upper rooms. Her duties and sense of responsibility take her in and out of the barn twenty times. After the pageant she stands beside the lily pond "between two fluidities," air and water, her feet on the earth, contemplating the lily pads which seem in her imagination to be the continents of the world, "islands of security, glossy and thick," touched by the air creature the dragonfly and nudged from below by the golden orfe. She strains to concentrate, to unite the disparate sections of her domain (148). Lucy is part bird; her "darlings," as much her children as little George and baby Caro, are the fish in the pond (149, 21).

Alpha and Omega, the beginning and the end, are sometimes represented in art as a bird and a fish.[40] But to believe they are the same is to deny life with its constant regeneration (T 353). And religion, in the person of Lucy who is Themis, although she is a unifier, represents an old order, an order no longer appropriate, as Bart recognises, for the modern world: "How imperceptive her religion made her! The fumes of that incense obscured the human heart" (147). Here Woolf rejects any accepted moral code for the moral lesson of La Trobe, the writer of epics who wants no formal thanks, for she seeks inspiration for the words of her next play. La Trobe's moments of glory never make her complacent: "Glory possessed her—for one moment" because, as Harrison tells us, "To the real creative artist even praise and glory are swallowed up in the supreme joy of creation" (151, AR 213). Virginia Woolf's own view was that a "new book . . . not only thrusts its predecessor from the nest but has a way of subtly blackening its character in comparison with its own."[41]

Encouraging communion at an assembly of the populace or at an intimate meal for family and friends is, in mythology, the responsibility of Themis the convener. Frequently in Virginia Woolf's fiction a meal is a literary device by which she groups her characters in preparation for the plot which follows or grows out of that sacramental feast. The luncheon party at Pointz Hall is central to the novel. The characters begin the mysterious interchange of emotion and reason and the pooling of their wisdom in the dining room, a space with no location in time, "a shell singing of what was before time was" (31). Woolf likens the room to a vase, the central symbol of Isis: a vase in which lie the beginnings of wisdom and the fertilizing power of the moon goddess. Within the silent, empty room wait passively, showing neither hope nor despair, the symbols of life, love and generation: a bowl of red, white and yellow roses interspersed with sword- and heart-shaped leaves and painted images of a nameless woman and a man with a name, a horse and a dog. In a few sentences Woolf suggests the history of the world and a possible future: the silent, mysterious and anonymous woman; the proprietary man who "held the rein in his hand"; the rose, symbol of pure love; and sword- and heart-shaped leaves, symbols of generation. All are held within the vase which is Isis, Mother and life (30).

Candish, the oddly named family butler who arranges the tableau in the dining room before lunch, provides another instance of the comic verbal shorthand by which Woolf unites vast philosophies and ideologies by reducing them to two syllables and personifying them in a single character. The name of the butler represents the irreverent satire of Voltaire's *Candide* combined with the loving compassion of the goddess Ishtar: "Queerly, he loved flowers, considering his gambling and drinking" (30). Candish's unexpected love of roses is Ishtar's; his curved, moon-shaped brush sweeps away dry crumbs and spares the fallen rose petals (154). Candide, in Paris with the Abbé from Périgord, gambles away 50,000 francs in two games of cards.[42] Candish's mother, one of the Perrys—perry is fermented pear juice—links him to drinking and, like Lucy Swithin, to Bacchus (59). The connection with Bacchus or Dionysos is strengthened through the great Hagia Triada Sarcophagos dated about 1500 B.C. and housed since 1903 in the museum at *Can*dia on the island of Crete where Jane Harrison and others made important discoveries about pre-Olympic religion. The sarcophagos sums up the significance of the ceremonies of ancient spring festivals, the sacrifices and sanctities all directed toward what Harrison calls "the bridal of the Earth and Sky, the New Birth of the World" (T 179).

The new birth of the world is just what Virginia Woolf posits in the final words of *Between the Acts*. She shares Voltaire's mistrust of the optimistic notion that all is for the best in "this best of all possible worlds."[43] Mrs. Manresa's opinion, "this ripe, this melting, this adorable world," is more qualified, more open to possibilities than that of Voltaire's Pangloss (45). So across centuries, wiping out chronological time, Candish draws together the Age of Reason and Ishtar, the force of nature controlling the cycle of life, in a vision of change through cooperation which is less utopian than it is faintly hopeful, depending as it does on our shifting perspectives as the new inheritors of technology. Acceptance of things as they are under the aegis of church, state and military is not enough. There must be hope and the continuing search for Candide's Cunégonde and the vision she represents that change will come if we " 'go and work in the garden,' " in this case the fertile medium of the mind of the artist who is at work in the garden of Pointz Hall at the crucial suspended time between the past and the future—between the acts.[44]

Mrs. Manresa and William Dodge, two intruders from the city, are among the group that settles down to filet of sole, cherry tart and champagne. Giles, Isa's husband and "the father of her children," a description she seems to prefer, comes late to lunch dressed as a cricketer—one who strikes blows—and blows, as do Manresa and Dodge, into the "sheltered harbour" of Pointz Hall and its centre, the place of sacramental communion, the dining room (34, 38).

The symbols of life and of unity are to be ingested with the entrée. The semitransparent soles (or souls) are helpfully coated, before cooking, by Mrs. Sands: with flour, ground from Demeter's corn; with egg, the symbol of the world, originally thought of as the moon and later split into earth and moon and another version of the great mother; and with crumbs from the dry crusts, masculine reason and logic, stored in the great earthenware crock, the vessel of the earth mother and a below-stairs, kitchen version of the aristocratic vase of the upper floor, the dining room.

Mrs. Manresa, "wild child of nature" who first met Giles at a cricket match, completes the goddess trinity at the table. She is "Lady of the Wild Things," the earth mother described by Jane Harrison as the mother of all living creatures. Manresa is earth mother, corn mother, and mature woman: "Like a goddess buoyant, abundant, . . . her cornucopia running over," she is of the earth, earthy; she rolls in the grass, weaves baskets, yodels among the hollyhocks (89, 35). The hollyhock, at one time, was known as the resurrection plant. Harrison argues the influence of the mythical mother and maid on the social order of ancient Athens. Demeter, "the prosperous, genial corn-mother" is physical, of the upper air; Kore or Persephone, the daughter or maiden, is more spiritual, of the underworld.[45]

The earth mother as Demeter, Zeus's wife, is at home in the patriarchal atmosphere of Olympus. Manresa effortlessly establishes an affinity with Bart and Giles; at teatime in the barn, she moves regally, yet as an equal among the gentry and the villagers, male and female. Manresa has traveled the world. Born on another continent, she wears jewels dug from the earth by a husband who may or may not be Ralph Manresa, a Jew. Although she is of the "upper air" Manresa has a night life: she strolls the garden at midnight, her past life a mystery. Her grandfather had been imprisoned *down under* in Tasmania. Her exclamation, "You don't know my husband!" supposedly refers to his generosity with money, or his foolish philanthropy (Ralph in dialect means a fool) but on a different level refers to the helmet of invisibility, also possessed by Bart in his youth, that he wears as Hades, lord of the underworld (17). Hades owns the gems and riches below the earth and of course the jewels Manresa wears on her fingers, the jewels of Ishtar (146). Manresa has the clear-sightedness made possible by the brilliance of the full moon: "Ralph when he was at the war, couldn't have been killed without her seeing him," for the moon lights all the earth and the dead are Demeter's people (36).

Although the corn goddess must appease Apollo the sun god if her crops are to ripen, the evening sun does not suit the makeup of this wild child of nature: "plated it looked, not deeply interfused' (196). In "Tintern Abbey" Wordsworth writes of a presence "deeply interfused" in nature, refers to the "shooting lights" in the "wild eyes" of his sister, and goes on to instruct her "let the moon / Shine on thee in thy solitary walk."[46] So Manresa, lady of the wild things, jewels rather than eyes flashing red and green light, hides her real presence beneath an easy social manner, a manner that impresses men but fails to convince women, "for they being conspirators, saw through it." (128, 34). As human beings developed from hunters to agriculturists the lady of the wild things became of necessity Demeter the goddess of the cultivated earth. The maid and queen of the underworld is Demeter's child, but also part of her. Because her seed must die before it breaks from the earth to bloom, Demeter's dark side, her sorrow is never far beneath the surface:[47] in the recognition of the finale of the pageant "for an instant tears ravaged her powder" (137).

Thoughts of death then are never far from signs of life in *Between the Acts*. Manresa brings fresh life to the lunch party: champagne, soma, the drink of the moon goddess, will restore youth to Old Bart (34). Manresa "ogles" Candish the butler, conferring sexuality on the "stuffed man" who understands her need for a corkscrew. One does not, of course, use a corkscrew to open champagne. The wild child of nature cocks her thumb as she opens the bottle; the corkscrew suggests the phallus needed to renew the earth (33).[48] On the terrace after lunch Manresa stirs the coffee, cream and brown sugar candy mixture "sensuously, rhythmically . . . round and round" in her cup, another form of the regenerating cauldron, the candy congealing, uniting with the cream, the richest part of the milk (44). Milk was thought to be, when water was scarce, an effective sacrifice to induce the moon goddess who was heavenly cow to send rain to the earth.[49] At the tea interval Isa pours a mug of milk for George, her little boy, as he swims blindly toward her against the waves of obstructing skirts and trousers of the indifferent crowd of villagers. She offers him life or courage to continue, as Woolf herself continued to live and write "against the current" and "the world's notorious indifference."[50]

In Plutarch's legend of Isis and Osiris the story is told of the child Maneros the fisher, another version of the archetypal, ailing, regenerative god, who fell overboard as he beheld with awe Isis' grief at the death of Osiris.[51] Maneros means understanding of love; Manresa stirs cream into the revivifying cup of coffee. Skill with the written word is not her forte; she chatters, perhaps like a magpie, another magic bird. But her intentions are good. She has Shakespeare "by heart" if not by rote; she is a life giver connected, it seems by name, to little George, the new generation for whom Isa must reject death and free the vision of love in her poems for him to understand (44). Woolf referred to the writing of *Between the Acts* as an attempt at a new method, "a richer pat."[52] She, in her way, is milking her imagination, pouring it out upon the ground as a sacrifice, a libation in the form of words to irrigate and give life to dry and dusty literature. Clearly Woolf's use of words is impressively economical; each word resembles in its multiplicity the starlings "syllabling discordantly life, life, life," which attack the tree behind which Miss La Trobe hides to preserve her anonymity (152).

Woolf ridiculed in *Three Guineas* the lifeless words of men, accusing men of having "no soul with which to preach and no mind with which to write." Indeed to listen to a lecture by an Englishman was akin to medieval torture.[53] The dark underground caves of Manresa in the Spanish Pyrenees were the setting in 1525 for the writings of Ignatius Loyola the founder of the Jesuits, whose paradoxical rule demanded complete submission to the idea of hierarchical infallibility in matters of faith, while advocating reason and logic in education. Modern totalitarian brainwashing techniques and Orwellian doublethink are not very different from the teaching methods of the Jesuit schoolmasters of upper- and middle-class European boys. "If," says Loyola, "the church teaches to be black what the eye sees as white, the mind will believe it to be black."[54] Although the dark cave nurtured Jesuit ultramontanism, Manresa the goddess of moonlight, the earth and the underworld, herself a symbolic womb, can conceive a new world even after four hundred years of suppression of feminine wisdom and values.

Ignatius wrote his book of spiritual exercises and in spite of the darkness of the cave came to see all things in a new light, crossed the desert to Jerusalem on a donkey, and eventually returned to Spain to found his order of priests. He learned Latin with the help of a woman, Isabel Roser, then founded a home for Jews converted to Christianity and another for women of disorderly life. It must have been a great joke for Woolf to give the name of Ignatius's pious lady teacher to one of her own goddess heroines and the name of his place of spiritual inspiration to another: the somewhat disorderly woman married for Woolf's purposes to Ralph Manresa, the Jew converted not to the church but to riches and the status of the English landed gentry.

Manresa's companion William Dodge appears to be a gentleman. His presence disturbs, raises questions which he avoids answering directly. Manresa's relationship with him is ambiguous. Jane Harrison describes the relation of matriarchal goddesses to their male companions as "half-way between Mother and Lover with a touch of the Patron saint." These gracious creatures required their heroes to do great deeds for them in return for protection.[55] Dodge is no hero. In contrast Giles seems so to Manresa: "Somehow she was the Queen; and he (Giles) was the surly hero" (71). Dodge is slippery as a snake, "unwholesome," "half-man," keeping hidden what is sinister: his left hand in his pocket is "firmly if surreptitiously" closed as he endeavors to fit himself into a society that has no special niche for him (32, 57, 83).

Dodge's expert adjustment of Isa's deck chair reflects how much better he has learned to adjust than she who hides her deviant side, her artistry within the rigid covers of an account book. "She held her deck chair at the wrong angle. The frame with the notches was upside down" (41). Dodge cannot hide his twisted face as he does his left hand: Isa and Giles guess his secret. Giles, who obeys the rules of society, is enraged. He can conform to expectations with military precision. He "nicked his chair into position with a jerk" (43). Dodge considerately unfolds Isa's chair and fixes the bar "into the right notch," as he has learned to fit himself, unobtrusively, into a society whose arbitrary categories cannot really contain him. He appreciates Isa's discomfort with the "myriad of hair thin ties" of proper domesticity (18). Aesthete rather than artist, Dodge obtains pleasure from the contemplation of art rather than joy from its creation.

Jane Harrison distinguishes the practical man of action from the aesthete who desires sensation and who, when he does not feel, cannot bring himself to act. At the most he can simulate action by the contemplation of beauty—beauty in relation to the way he would like to feel but cannot. Dodge asks, "Beauty—isn't that enough?" (64). The true artist feels strongly and sees clearly and is forced to speak, paint or write as does La Trobe and to a lesser extent Isa. Giles is inarticulate and so responds to his feelings by violent action, by stamping out the perverted and incompatible union of the snake and the toad he finds "couched in the grass" (75).[56]

Dodge alone is cold, unable to acknowledge his forbidden sexual feelings for Giles and able only to simulate emotion in response to the painting of the beautiful woman in the dining room. His unfeeling, critical eye is upon Isa as she recites her poetry. "Always some cold eye crawled over the surface like a winter blue-bottle!" (128).[57] Although Dodge affects an appreciation of the skill of the artist, carefully trying to prejudge what he should or should not say, he cannot rouse feelings he has never had and cannot stir emotion long ago deadened by the repression of his sexuality. Giles knew "what his left hand was doing" and calls Dodge truly "a fingerer of sensations" (83, 48). Harrison suggests the aesthete, most often unsuccessfully, "seeks the sensation of stirring" his senses (AR 214).

Dodge, a misfit in the male-defined world, sees it sullied as it sees him, as he was made to see it as a child, his head held beneath dirty water. He is not happily man or woman; neither is he satisfiedly androgynous. He is William the invader of the enclosed world of Pointz Hall, yet he is no conquering hero. Ge or Gaia the earth mother spoke ancient wisdom at the oracle of Dodona to the dove priestesses couched in the grass, their ears to the earth, as the olive green snake is couched for Giles to crush with his shoe (T 389). William Dodge is named, in Virginia Woolf's whimsical lexicography, for the male conquerer of England and for the oracular shrine Dodona and the earth mother Ge, as well as for the evasive or dodgy behaviour by which he survives.

Neither can one avoid allusion to Dickens's Artful Dodger, he who fingered lightly the contents of pockets in *Oliver Twist*. In Woolf's turned-around universe

Dodge's twisted face, attraction to the Oliver family, and Bill, the diminutive form of his name, merge conventional good with deviance and with the evil of Dickens's Bill Sykes; they merge male power with female wisdom in a character for whom a place must be made in the reincarnate world. Dodge is "a toady; a lick spittle; . . . a flickering, mind-divided little snake in the grass," symbolically crushed underfoot by Giles (48, 57). Yet he is "healed" by Lucy Swithin, not of his unhappiness—happiness is not Woolf's point—but of his alienation. Lucy, whose winter home is at Hastings where William invaded England in 1066, the best known date in the English history in which she does not believe, welcomes Dodge into the house, the center of life, to show him through the upper rooms to the nursery.

If the big room with the windows open to the garden is the antechamber to the place of prophetic utterance, and the empty dining room contains within its marble coldness the symbols of the past and of future life, the nursery, its door open to anyone, holds the elements that can nourish the new world. Dodge has passed through the meeting place, the morning room, and the place of conception and birth, the bedroom, to the "cradle of the race." Words, instruments of "a thousand possibilities," can menace Giles the man of conventional action (47). To Dodge the aesthete, they raise themselves as symbols of a world that will have a place for him when he is reborn.

The nursery is warm and moist; the anonymous, unframed, mass-produced image of the Newfoundland dog pinned to the wall does not require critical assessment, for the dog represents the god of speech for the common people. It is worth noting that Byron had a monument at Newstead Abbey inscribed with a poem in praise of Boatswain, a Newfoundland dog. Boatswain, or in common parlance Bo'sun, is a ship's officer. Phonetically similar to Boss or Bossy, Bo'sun is really Miss La Trobe, the creator of a new language *and* "a commander pacing his deck" (49).[58] In the new-found land of children the dog is simply a good friend, known for its sagacity, good temper and the strong swimming ability needed to keep afloat, head above water, in that watery microcosm Pointz Hall. The rocking horse, a nineteenth-century invention, is child-sized recalling the real horse replaced through modern technology by the motor car. The empty cot, the nurse's abandoned sewing, the toy horse, barely still, the open door all suggest a holding of the breath, a temporary suspension of the process of life until the "crew" returns, ready to play the second act.

Dodge, with Lucy's help, can keep his head above water, but there is nothing in Lucy to "weight a man like Giles to the earth" (87). He needs solid, earthy Manresa so that he may "keep his orbit" for he is Osiris and Apollo, the sun who brings Demeter's crops to flower and to fruition (89). Giles the inarticulate hero, like Wagner's Parsifal the pure or guileless fool, must ask the question that will free the world from pain. Manresa speaks and sings but cannot write, yet both he and she are needed to give life to literature, "common ground" where all must "trespass freely and fearlessly." Woolf's point, clearly made in "The Leaning Tower," is that literature can only survive by crossing the "gulf" between the formally educated—upper- and middle-class men—and the uneducated—women and the poor. Beyond that gulf as Giles knows, murder is committed; minds are fettered by ignorance (39).

Giles the questing hero, manacled like Theseus to a rock in hell and "forced passively to behold indescribable horror," must find a way to communicate his anger and concern (48). The affinity he and Manresa feel for each other, while on one level the affinity of the burgeoning earth for the light and warmth of the sun, is also the affinity needed between the formally educated professional classes whose "uniform" Giles wears at dinner and the working classes with whom Manresa is so comfortable. In the reborn world there will be an easing of the frustrations and unhappiness afflicting Isa, Dodge, Giles and Manresa—the symbolic present generation caught between two worlds, "one dying, the other struggling to be born." Little George and his sister baby Caro can grow up without the restrictions of lofty elitism and frustrated impotence found in a life divided by patriarchal "hedges."[59]

Woolf's metaphorical hedges, personified in Rupert Haines—recall that "hain" is Old English for hedge—diminish for Isa as she makes her choice between death and life: " 'Now I follow' (she pushed her chair back. . . . The man in grey was lost in the crowd by the ilex) 'that old strumpet' (she invoked Mrs. Manresa's tight, flowered figure in front of her) 'to have tea' " (73). Giles hedged about only by custom and convention, not really by his personality, shows many possibilities. Woolf has given him Lytton Giles Strachey's second name, suggesting that literary talent and homosexual love are not beyond him. Certainly he knows William Dodge is attracted to him. But Dodge's secret is safe. Charlemagne is said to have told, under the seal of the confessional, a "secret sin" to his favorite priest, an abbot named Giles.[60] Giles is also Farmer Giles the prototypal yeoman of England, deflected from his preferred occupation by modern life: "Given his choice he would have chosen to farm" (38). Rupert Haines, on the other hand, is a gentleman farmer, representing Byron's "race worn out quite," ready to disappear as Haines does later, leaving Isa free like Woolf to follow her own furrow: "There he was for one second; but surrounded, inaccessible, and now vanished" (113).[61]

Rupert Haines is the only threatening male figure in the novel. Giles, the guileless fool, and even foolish Ralph Manresa are lost and questing heroes needed for the new plot, the unlived, unwritten history of the second act. Giles, like Parsifal, wears black in the final scene of the novel, as he plays the part dredged up by La Trobe from the muddy depths of her mind. According to ancient Egyptian myth, the snake and toad emerged from chaos; the toad or frog, self-created from the mud of the Nile; the snake, female, with an affinity for the depths of the earth.[62] The monstrous embrace, an inversion that can never give life, implies not only sterility but genocide.

Giles's violent reaction is immature, but affirms his desire for life over death. He strides to the barn, the temple of the goddesses; Mrs. Manresa has "vaguely some sense that he had proved his valour for her admiration" (81). To Isa, his sacrifice is an offering without merit, for it accomplishes nothing new: he is playing games, "a silly little boy with blood on his boots" (84). If Giles is the hero Gilgamesh (another linguistic possibility), his attempt to overcome the goddess Ishtar is bound to fail, for like the moon she cannot be possessed.[63] Wagner's Parsifal washed his feet before entering the castle of the grail to heal Amfortas; Giles changes his blood-stained tennis shoes for black patent leather pumps before he speaks his fateful words (156).

Giles has then, historical, mythical and literary significance. When he arrives for lunch in his cricketer's play clothes, he quickly eats his fish so that no one waits for the cherry tart which follows. Manresa recites a child's rhyme over the uneaten cherry seeds, establishing herself as a ploughboy or Demeter ready to walk over the fertile earth; Bart, a thief according to his seeds, is Hades, abductor of Persephone. Before dessert is served Bart catches a glimpse of a figure in white in the garden: the scullery maid or perhaps a ghost. Jane Harrison tells us that the Greek spring festival includes ceremonies for placating the dead (T 275). The fear of ghosts is allayed by the certainty of reincarnation. Whether the ghost is a lady in white as imagined by the scullery maid, or the sheep whose thigh bone was dragged from the lily pond, makes no difference to a totemistic people who mentally fuse humans with other creatures, as Lucy Swithin does when it takes her "five seconds in actual time, in mind time ever so much longer" to separate Grace the parlor maid from a dinosaur (11).

The meal left by the Greeks for souls to be reborn consisted of seeds, cooked but not eaten, to be taken by the dead to the netherworld, given body, and sent up for harvest in the familiar cycle of regeneration of the earth. An ancient ceremony for the raising of ghosts required the sacrifice of an animal, sometimes a sheep.[64] The cooked cherry stones, the sheep's thigh bone, the flash of white, the talk of ghosts are all vestiges of "actual time" long past, but also of "mind time" which is, in the chronological sense, timeless, and thus present at Pointz Hall to re/mind us, with the help of La Trobe's artistic vision the pageant, how we may invent the plot and speak our parts for the remainder of our existence: in "mind time," eternity.

Lucy Swithin's "two minds" diverge further. They flutter away like pigeons as she leans, in the inviting attitude of Ishtar the compassionate virgin prostitute, from her upstairs window overlooking the crescent-shaped gravel driveway on which the audience assembles before the play begins. (58).[65] The audience "streaming" and "spreading" through the grounds of Pointz Hall represents the class strata of England, all of whom, servants, landowners, writers, clergy, (insiders, outsiders and commoners in Woolf's terms) fit into a "system that did not shut out," for all have something to contribute and to learn.[66] Again Woolf's analogy is to the common ground of literature. The audience of the pageant tramples on flowers and "bruise[s] a lane on the grass" just as she suggests will happen when commoners claim their right to familiarity with the classics: "Aeschylus, Shakespeare, Virgil, and Dante . . . would say: 'read me, read me for yourselves.' . . . Of course . . . we shall trample many flowers and bruise much ancient grass" (146).[67]

Among the middle-class spectators is Cobbet of Cobb's Corner, a conservative newcomer to the community who grows and nurtures prize flowers. He is "not an asset," self-sufficient—he does his own housework and is a solitary individual, an observer of human behaviour and not inclined to mingle with the common herd (58).

William Cobbett, popular journalist and political reformer of the early nineteenth century was at once radical and reactionary. He wanted, by radical political means, to establish his reactionary ideal of a rural England where all classes would live in harmony on the land: a naïve ambition that showed little understanding of a complex issue.[68] Cobbett loved the English countryside and people but had lived for a time in France, and along with other self-taught readers and writers among working-class radicals of his day, had certainly read Voltaire.[69] A critical journalist, he was so prickly that he earned the name Peter Porcupine.[70] William Hazlitt wrote of him, "William Cobbett strips himself quite as naked as anybody could wish," a qualified assessment suggesting something held back.[71] The truth, in Woolf's terms, is revealed by stripping away the layers that disguise us. But the truth leaves no defense. " 'It's a good day, some say, the day we are stripped naked. Others, it's the end of the day' " (114). Women who are forced to tell the truth, remove their disguises, play their unacted part, unleash so much power that there may be a "brawl in the barrack room" (115).

Cobbet of Cobb's Corner is, it seems, a dull man of integrity. He observes the socially determined female behavior of Mrs. Manresa as she plays her "little game" and characterizes it "human nature." Plants, he feels, have integrity (83). But Cobbet cannot connect plants with humans. His ideals of perfection leave no room for disorderly emotions. He preserves all that is rare and perfect, discourages the rank growth of the rain forest. Retired from the hot, dry plains of India, his habit is to ration water, to dole it out according to schedule to his cultivated, cultured plants. "Cobbet had out his watch. Three hours till seven, he noted; then water the plants" (75). Cobbet's timepiece, a symbol of the Age of Reason, sets him, as the tape measure and newspaper set Bart, where facts and figures give security and restrict imagination.

He sits alone beneath the symbolic, unclimbable monkey puzzle tree and ponders La Trobe's motive for mystifying her audience, for encouraging them to climb her tree. Cobbet sits beneath the tree for he worships at the foot of reason. The grinning monkey face of Europe's intellectual master peers from the prickly branches of the genus Araucaria, native to Chile and the mountainous area of Peru, over which Candide was lifted by a marvelous machine imagined by Voltaire.[72]

Miss La Trobe, Woolf's comic, artistic genius more than Voltaire, with her machine the gramophone ticking in the bushes, can push her audience at least part way to the top of the tree from where they may clearly see the route to continue their journey. Cobbet digs in his garden; he has heeded Voltaire's advice to "go and work in the garden," but along with Giles, he represents the conventional and cautious masculine mind, a challenge to La Trobe: "she saw Giles Oliver with his back to the audience. Also Cobbet of Cobb's Corner. She hadn't made them see. It was a failure, another damned failure!" (74) La Trobe's single purpose is unity. Giles and Cobbet must not be allowed to "slip the noose" (91).

A cobb is a male swan. Joseph Wright's dialect dictionary, well known to Virginia Woolf, defines a cobb as a mixture of straw, lime, gravel and clay to make walls. Cobbet is then connected with Rupert Haines who Isa imagines as a swan, and who builds hedges rather than walls. But Cobbet is also an element in the adhesive mixture on La Trobe's boss or plasterer's tray. So there is hope for Cobbet as an individual, for his vision although limited and reactionary is a vision of life. La Trobe can help him to grow a more luxuriant and colorful garden if she can draw him out of his isolation into the circle of her art.

Another who will benefit from La Trobe's artistic vision—the funds from the pageant are to illuminate his church and to rebuild its "perpetually falling steeple"—is the Reverend G. W. Streatfield, the personification of England's Georges and Williams, city streets and rural fields (22, 129, 140). Streatfield, a "strapping clergyman," who carries leafy hurdles, props for the play, holds moral and religious beliefs that bring him close to the primitive or totemistic society where group life and collective consciousness cause the suffering or prosperity of one member to affect all in the group (58). Religious practices and beliefs are remnants of ritual and beliefs from a social structure buried in antiquity (AR 86, 87).

In *Three Guineas* Woolf specified ridicule for the clergy. Her scarcely tolerant description of Streatfield focuses on his ineptitude with language, his inability to bring any new ideas to his congregation. Yet "one fact mitigated the horror; his forefinger was stained with tobacco juice." Although Streatfield is an anachronism: "a piece of traditional church furniture; a corner cupboard; or the top beam of a gate, fashioned by generations of carpenters after some lost-in-the-mists-of-antiquity model," he "wasn't such a bad fellow" (138). Linguistically, as Judy Little observes, Streatfield may be a straight field closed by the white gate of his restrictive clergyman's collar, itself suggestive of the straight or narrow gate of the gospels (Luke 13:24, Matt. 7:13–14).[73] But streat, an obsolete form of street, originally stratos, suggests the city; and the field is the domain of the peasant or countryman of which peisant is an older form.

So we see in Streatfield not only the benign Anglican clergyman with a tobacco-stained yellow forefinger—yellow is a color of spring and of renewal, tobacco a drug suggesting self-indulgence—but Peisistratos the benevolent Greek tyrant of antiquity who understood the need for emotion and for Dionysos in the restricted world of commerce, the city. The representative of Christ the carpenter is, through his more distant antecedents, a natural man, one who, at La Trobe's behest, carries leafy hurdles; to him Themis is one with the natural order as she was to the Greeks: he is ready to perform the dithyramb, the leaping dance of the spring celebration of new birth, to leap over his hurdles for "goodly Themis" as La Trobe's spectacle begins (T 535).

At the centre of the front row of spectators in the ancient Dionysiac theatre, the priest of Dionysos sat between the priest of Apollo the laurel bearer and the priest of Olympian Zeus (AR 11). On the lawn in front of the terrace at Pointz Hall "in the very centre" sits Mrs. Manresa, earth mother and moon goddess and "Queen of the Festival," flanked by Giles the guileless hero and old Bart who sees morality in reason rather than in nature (61, 61). Lucy Swithin, the religious principle itself, arrives late and takes her place next to her brother. Dodge and Isa, aesthete and artist, sit close together among the dignitaries. The man in grey and his wife, late because of a breakdown on the road, sit several rows back; they have no priestly function. As in ancient Athens, the front row is occupied by officials of the state, those with priestly authority to administer sacraments.

Among them, fittingly, "looking fluid and natural" is Bond the cowman, the only character who moves smoothly between animals and humans (60). Bond is Hathor's priest, a figure symbolic of the heavenly cow goddess's task, about to begin, of binding together into a community the wildly incompatible individuals who as actors mimic the past yet live in the present, and those as audience who are present to watch La Trobe's parade of the past.

3

Pageant

*All consciousness is a preservation and accumulation of the past in
the present. . . . All consciousness is an anticipation of the
future. . . . Consciousness is above all a hyphen, a tie between the
past and future.*

Henri Bergson, *Life and Consciousness*

The scope of the pageant is vast, covering in twenty-five minutes of "actual time"
ancient Britain and Chaucerian and Elizabethan England. The Age of Reason, the
Victorian era, present-time 1939, and two intervals occupy another hour-
and-a-half. The amateur actors forget their lines; the script is "skimble-
skamble stuff"; the programme, written on "blurred carbon paper," is as difficult
to understand as the mysterious message puzzling Cobbet and Streatfield (72).
Virginia Woolf's survey of England's past is less cursory than it is commodious.
The brief, broken-up scenes carry, like the rest of the novel, multiple references,
sometimes humorous, sometimes savagely ironic, to English history and literature
and myths from ancient cultures which can make us, caught unprepared, see
clearly our mirrored selves.

La Trobe puts the actors and the audience at the mercy of the elements by
holding the pageant out-of-doors rather than in the barn. The dressing room in the
bushes, the green room of modern theatre and anteroom to the terrace, the place of
spectacle, generates butterfly catching or inspires creativity. Bartholomew, Lucy
and Giles have all chased and tried to capture the many-hued butterflies, symbolic
of the psyche, the soul, the creative spirit. Just lately little George, the inheritor,
has netted a cabbage white, a common variety, a sign of change (45, 50). Up and
down the terrace barred by leaning birch trees reminiscent of Woolf's leaning
tower, La Trobe, on the ground with the masses, paces and studies her script (49,
50).

About 1897, Virginia Woolf read Hakluyt's *Voyages* and decided to model
herself on the Elizabethans. Twenty years later her enthusiasm for the age was

undiminished and seemingly perfectly compatible with her involvement in the world of ancient Greece and the work of Jane Harrison.[1] Woolf's image of the writers of the 1930s, secure in their leaning tower yet longing to be "down on the ground with the mass of human kind" suggests, feminist writer Brenda Silver argues, the outdoor Elizabethan playhouse and direct audience participation in the drama.[2] Yet behind the hyperbole and broad humor of Elizabethan writing lay the consciousness of death waiting in the wings or, Woolf tells us, "a sense of the presence of the Gods."[3] La Trobe's pageant is permeated with the sense of the mystery-god Dionysos, all-pervasive and impossible to intellectualize or to capture in an individual character (T 476). La Trobe, the creator, has not yet found a way to fuse butterflies, light, laughing mothers and energetic children, so she fails to find inspiration for her next work: "'No I don't get it,' she muttered" (50). First she must try to reveal her vision to the audience assembled to watch the pageant.

The pageant, largely plotless as Elizabethan plays were not, forces communal participation and rouses indefinable emotion. Little England of the prologue, Phyllis Jones, is etymologically akin to Philomela, the nightingale and ravished sister of Procne the swallow, one of Lucy Swithin's roles. Isis, a part played by Lucy and by Isa, turned herself into a swallow to search for the body of Osiris, killed by Set, the ruler of the desert and husband of Isis' sister Nephthys, meaning end or victory, who was considered to be at the extreme edge of the desert, seldom touched by the fertile waters of the Nile. Bart wonders how his sister could have borne children; Isis never found the phallus of Osiris after Set tore him into fourteen pieces.[4] Osiris was reborn without the means of procreation; Woolf is concerned for the rape and future sterility of England and of English literature. The arrival of the man in grey and his wife emphasises the air of doom: Death and Nemesis cannot be long put off by a ruse, even a breakdown on the road (63).

The prologue to the pageant, spoken by a childish England, is followed by scenes of an England, powerful, almost invincible under Elizabeth I. Woolf's admiration for the Elizabethans is reflected in her character Eliza Clark from the village shop: "eminent, dominant," she glows with the strength and vigor of the golden age. Her physical strength, as well as the soapbox, puts her above the bearded men she rules; her loud voice ensures that her words cannot be blown away on the breeze or lost amid laughter and applause. But the twentieth-century Eliza forgets the words of the first Elizabeth. Giles the guileless fool speaks, to the same tune as Eliza, the words of Lear gone mad: "I fear I am not in my perfect mind."[5] He in turn forgets the words of Elizabeth's poet, and Albert the village idiot cheerfully and confidently takes the stage.

Albert, all the letters of his name but the *O* of indivisible time contained in La Trobe, is in the tradition of Shakespeare's clowns and jesters (William Dodge comments that he is in the tradition). His title idiot—the Freudian id, the missing *I* of Voltaire, the *O* of eternity and Io a Grecian cow goddess worshiped in Egypt as Isis—gives him unexpected dimensions. He seems to be a catalyst and a scapegoat for the other characters (83). Lear's fool complains that he is whipped for telling the truth, for lying and sometimes for keeping quiet.[6] Natural in his part, Albert needs no dressing up for "mopping and mowing" (66). Woolf refers here to Shakespeare's Edgar as poor Tom, supposedly host to the fiend Flibbertigibbet of mopping and mowing, the possessor of chambermaids and waiting women.[7] Albert causes great discomfort among the villagers. He may do "something dreadful," for he is a primitive trickster figure, childlike and uninhibited. Yet because his behavior is instinctive, he reflects the hidden urges of genteel Mrs. Elmhurst, who covers her eyes rather than risk seeing that which unites her with chambermaids and with the idiot (67).

The plot of the next scene, played in front of Queen Elizabeth who is really Eliza Clark, is one of loss and discovery, of old age making way for younger life. The details are not clear even through Mrs. Winthrop's lorgnettes. The actors are difficult to hear; the plot matters little. If it begets emotion, that is enough: "All else was verbiage, repetition," says Isa (70). Aged Elsbeth (a form of Elizabeth and Isabella) sickens and dies, making way for her child the young prince, played by Albert Perry—primitive and Bacchanalian—and Sylvia Edwards playing a duke's daughter who had been lost in a cave. Silvia, mother of Romulus, gave birth in a cave and concealed her child in a basket among rushes to save him from the wrath of her uncle who wished him killed.[8] Elsbeth asks forgiveness from Mary in heaven for not slaying her child. The "sin" of preserving life is an ironic criticism of the violence perpetrated by the church. The church is represented in the scene by an inept priest whose cotton wool moustache makes his words impossible to understand.

Woolf melds "actual time" and "mind time" in Elsbeth the Crone—Kronos, reincarnation, and Chronos, time—played by Mrs. Otter of the End House (T 496). The otter is an amphibious beast who lives, like Isis's sister Nephthys, at the water's edge. Isa identifies with the withered Elsbeth by more than her name: "'There's little blood in my arm' Isabella repeated" (69). If she gives allegiance to the desert ruler, she may have to remain, like the otter, close to the source of fertility, longing for moisture to free her emotions and to keep alive her creativity. On the terrace after lunch she felt "a desire for water. 'A beaker of cold water, a beaker of cold water,' she repeated and saw water surrounded by walls of shining glass" (52). But it is difficult to remain constantly alert. She may through sheer weariness be coopted; "blunt arrows bruised her." She cannot easily distinguish between love and hate, attraction and revulsion (52). Apollo's blunt arrows were tipped with lead and designed to repel love.[9] So for Isa, desire for life "petered out, suppressed by the leaden duty she owed to others" (53). Elsbeth falls dead and becomes "she to whom all's one now, summer or winter," recalling the peaceful, grey plain of death, the underworld where dwell the shades, their personalities dulled and obscured (70).

Isa continues in the first interval, as the barn fills with people, to remind us of the agonizing task of communication and of the isolation of the artist who works alone in the dry, uninspirational atmosphere of middle-class England (78). The cook Trixie, Mrs. Sands, a "thin acid, woman, red-haired, sharp and clean, who never dashed off masterpieces," fails to notice the teeming animal and insect life in the barn Woolf ironically describes as "empty" (28, 76). She is blind to butterflies and moths, female creative power; mice, under the protection of Apollo in ancient times, do not exist for her.[10] Eyes expand and narrow in the semidarkness; the eyes of the Egyptian cat god Bastet, denoted the moon's waxing and waning;[11] the eyes of the myriad life in the barn also reflect the phases of the moon. Dry Mrs. Sands conserves her emotions exclusively for the worship of cats. Her red hair is treated with henna from the Egyptian privet, a hedge which keeps her from the fertile river water. Her nickname Trixie does not suit her, for it is derived from the ending of feminine agent nouns such as impera*trix*. She is a servant who follows orders and can never initiate action or be original. Until the disparate unite and literature comes from the anonymous, common voice, she will never, unlike La Trobe, seethe and simmer the broth of regeneration in her cooking pots, will never "dash off masterpieces."

Through contrasting the brittle, disturbing sounds of modern life with thoughts of the peace death can offer, Woolf emphasizes the dreadful nature of the work women must do to defy the desert rulers. Union with death could be preferable to the alienation Isa feels listening to the meaningless clatter of china and chatter of voices which become, in her imagination, "china faces glazed and hard" (78). After death, water would not inspire but cover and silence forever. However, Isa's offering of a pin dropped into the wishing well is not an effective sacrifice, for a well has no use for pins. To make contact with the gods you must establish a thread of communication like Mrs. Manresa's thread of sensation, or you must open yourself up somehow to the spirit or mana of the gods. Jane Harrison writes of the sweat lodge of the Algonquin Indians: sometimes the Indians would slit their skins with knives to allow free passage of the manitou.

Woolf's sweat lodge is the greenhouse: a tightly closed (the door must be kicked open), humid place where Isa and Giles take Dodge and Manresa to absorb the moisture that will "drive out everything that inflicts pain" (T 138). The otter must slip into the river to remain alive; human sexual, artistic, nurturing and civilizing qualities need strong drafts of mana to resist the death traps set by church, state and military. La Trobe the artist know this: "Every cell in her body was absorbent" (111). Isa opens her body to spiritual in/fluence by miming plunging a knife into her breast as she stands before the fig tree, symbolic of home and safety, and the hydrangea, meaning water vessel. She hands Dodge a geranium, named for the crane that brings the sign for rain and for ploughing, as they sit together beneath the vine sacred to Dionysos and to Osiris.

Dodge and Isa contemplate the shadow of death on their future: a clear pattern has yet to emerge from the crisscross lines in the vine leaf. Through the now-open door of the greenhouse, they hear three notes, A.B.C. "Someone was practising scales." The notes become first C.A.T., then "cat" (80). The sounds A.B.C. become musical symbols which become, in the minds of Isa and Dodge, the letters C.A.T. *T* does not exist in the musical scale, so the human capacity for symbolic thought transforms the sound into the image of an animal. Similarly the sounds of the scale become D.O.G. and then "dog" in the minds of Lucy and Bart (87). The images are those of Thoth the dog-faced Egyptian god of the moon, speech and the sciences, and of Bastet the cat, also sacred to the moon.[12] The words cat and dog are replaced by nursery rhymes spoken by an anonymous voice to a "simple" tune. The tune seems to soothe and calm the listeners, giving Dodge and Isa inspiration to speak plainly to each other, and Bart and Lucy equanimity to face their future with dignity.

Miss La Trobe frantically signals the "scraps and fragments" of the audience back to their seats, recalling Isis's desperate efforts to unite the pieces of Osiris's body. A voice asks the origin of Rabelais's expression "with a flea in his ear," suggesting the possibility of satire and coarse humour, as Mabel Hopkins, the Age of Reason in person, faces the audience (91).[13]

The Age of Reason and Enlightenment can be symbolically represented by a watch. The intricate, logical and reliable mechanism of irreversible time orders and gives meaning and purpose to life by dividing it neatly into periods of various lengths—days, hours, minutes—and gives the impression that life is controllable. Activities may be synchronised and the occurrence of certain events predicted by having faith in clock time, that is, in reason or logic. Extensions of reason are order, law and morality. Virginia Woolf opens avenues for us to explore possible changes we could make in the flawed system by which most people, calling it civilisation, consider they live. She introduces three scenes of outrageous parody of Restoration comedy in the tradition of Goldsmith and Sheridan by setting out as a sort of logogram of the peace and prosperity common to the eighteenth and nineteenth centuries, a china tea service.

La Trobe, as Lucy Swithin remarks, is able, like Racine, to indicate the plot with a single object and to concern herself with complexities of characters (104). She paints in words a picture of an age when the arts flowered as they only can in time of peace. But England's prosperity, and the power that discouraged attackers, came from riches extorted from remote places through the exploitation of unknown people. The theme of the eighteenth-century play may be read as regeneration. Woolf uses the Antipodes, as she uses Australia, as a metaphor for the underworld, the world against or beneath our feet. The role of the underworld is to restore life to the upper earth. A bitter irony gives nature's cornucopia to commerce: "in distant mines the savage sweats" and "Time, leaning on his sickle stands amazed" (92). The scenes are sprinkled with oblique references to mining, to "different ores" and to the industrialism that allowed the accumulation of great wealth and the rise of art and literature while it suppressed the voices of the poor and the uneducated.

A large clock controls the action in the second scene and the discussion in the third. The distinction between restrictive clock time and time as an emotional moment both instant and eternal is, for the purpose of the scene, the distinction between the attitudes of the old man and woman to whom money is more important than feelings, who have "passed the meridian," whose *time* is running out, and the heedless disregard for tiresome regulations of the younger pair who hasten to Gretna Green where one assumes they will conceive new life. Woolf's mythological references hark back to the Eastern religions to which many of the Greek gods owe their genesis (106).

Mrs. Otter of the End House appears again, "wonderfully made up" as Lady Harpy Harraden, Asphodilla or Sue. This time the child saved from death is her niece Flavinda, a "green girl" whose name comes from the Latin *flavin,* a yellow dye. Flavinda, "cast up in a lobster pot covered with seaweed," is reminiscent of Aphrodite, supposedly born from the sea, but originally an Oriental goddess identified with Ishtar.[14] Millie Loder (a lode is a vein of ore) plays Flavinda, uniting nature and technology.

Sir Spaniel Lilyliver, a cowardly dog, is a comic relative of Thoth the dog-faced Egyptian personification of the will that gives the tongue the power of speech.[15] He "rattles his tongue as a gambler rattles dice in a box" (94, 95). Lilyliver is afraid of poetry: "O done with rhymes. Rhymes are still-a-bed. Let's speak prose" (95). His attributes are those of the club-footed Greek god of fire, mining and metallurgy, Hephaestus, also an Eastern deity, to whom Aphrodite was married and frequently unfaithful. Sir Spaniel limps; his gouty foot feels like one of the burning horseshoes Hephaestus forges in his smithy.

Lilyliver's rival is Valentine, figuratively a rhyme in praise of romantic love. Valentine, Flavinda's lover, conceals himself in the clock, thereby becoming "the entrails of a timepiece," and by stopping the clock, successfully extends the time which is running out for the older couple (106). We are reminded of the literary continuum, the "thread of life" by which Isa and Giles "continue" Bart and Lucy. Lady Harpy, variously described by Sir Spaniel as Aphrodite, Aurora Borealis and the Sun is more accurately a "scritch owl, witch and vampire"—epithets less insulting than they seem (107).

In *Gyn/Ecology,* Mary Daly points out that witches were a knowledgeable, elite cross-section of the female population, and that the vampiristic rituals of the patriarchal religion reversed, in the blood-filled chalice, the original creative function associated with the cauldron of the priestess and later the witch.[16] When Sir Spaniel says "Pah! she stinks," he has noticed the characteristic stench of harpies, the mythic winged female scavengers and agents of the goddess Nemesis (99). Lady Harpy prefers to call herself Asphodilla, referring to the flower of death growing on the plains of Asphodel, and to the daffodil, the green and yellow flower of spring. She is a life giver. Not only does she nurture the green and yellow girl who will take her place in nature, but she passes on her skills to Deb her maid who is, significantly, someone unknown to the audience (94). As harpy, Asphodilla snatches Flavinda from the sea and snatches Deb from the hedge, saving both from death.

Deb like the harpy is a scavenger: of apple parings and crusts—discards from the earth's bounty of fruit and grain—from the table and of writing skills from her mistress's escritoire. Deb, her name a diminutive implying a debut, a beginning, signs her full name to the message she leaves as she escapes servitude for freedom "'What care I for your goose-feather bed? I'm off with the raggle-taggle gypsies O! Signed: Deborah, one time your maid.'" In biblical times Deborah, a prophetess and a woman of great spirit and courage, celebrated victory over the Canaanites by composing a canticle (Judg. 5).

On February 21, 1937, when Virginia Woolf was caught up in the work of *Three Guineas,* she wrote in her diary, "Today the reviewers have their teeth fixed in me; but what care I for a goose-feather bed etc."[17] She too, as prophet for the modern world, envisioned an age free of oppression and celebrated in literature and music. Deb represents the lower classes, the women inured to hardship and to criticism who will add their previously unknown voices to the common voice, injecting new life and writing new plots. Lady Harpy is not unduly distressed by her solitude, "sans niece, sans lover; and sans maid" (109). Woolf's parody is not as pessimistic or final as Shakespeare's "sans everything."[18]

The "green girl" cannot join with the gouty old man, or there will be no life. The servant, unlike Mrs. Sands of the desert, will "go over the hill" to become independent, to become equal and to stand with no hedge barring her from anyone, on the common ground. Asphodilla knows she has passed the meridian; the "game is over" when you are old. But Nemesis can be defied more effectively, told to keep her goose feathers to herself, if the *will* to change what some see as destiny is a collective one. Aunt, niece, lovers and servants are all elements in Woolf's grand design for regeneration.

The elemental spirit of birth has then many names. Dionysos roamed the world of the ancients under many titles before he came to Greece as the god of wine. Plain Sue and Brother Bob, children of an old-fashioned father who disliked foreign and fancy names, show traces of the god of an older drink than wine, the crude cereal intoxicant of Thrace and Egypt where Bromios and Sabazios were worshiped as gods of music and beer. Sue flirts a fan that might be the winnowing fan of the cereal god; Susan is a common English name for the hare, symbol of procreation and the moon. Bob was "emperor of the Indies," conquered by Dionysos in his eastern travels.[19]

Woolf puns outrageously on "Brother Bob's Will." The wilful young women defy the will of the ancient spirit of rebirth by choosing their own way, which will result in a renewed language. A language of the people will express better than the "shilling shockers" left by travellers in the library at Pointz Hall (hardly worth a "bob"), better than Isa's struggling poetry, the true feelings evoked by life: life threatened in the eighteenth century by mining and growing industrialism, in Woolf's day by the aeroplane, in ours by nuclear-powered missiles (13).

Halfway through the play, the unfamiliar and disturbing stage illusion is contrasted with a feeling, ironically evoked in the minds of the audience, of perfect order and truth. Wat the symbolic hare runs her courses; an evergreen tree and a clock set at three minutes to seven (the number of perfect order) suggest the harmony of nature and reason (100). Nature's "green girl" embraces her romantic lover *and* the "entrails of a timepiece" just as the clock strikes nine (the symbol of three worlds about to unite). Miss La Trobe "glowed with glory" as an unidentified voice supplies perspective with "'All that fuss about nothing.' "[20] The audience has seen and understood the simplicity and the beauty of a united world formed through the embrace of technology and nature with reason and love. For a moment, exhorting her actors to raise their voices, La Trobe becomes the god of speech: "she barked: 'Louder! Louder!' " For words, the instruments of truth, cannot be heard from the chorus. The primeval voices of the cows in the field take up the artistic burden in a cooperative gesture which strengthens the audience's perception of unity (102–4).

La Trobe's power—the power of Hathor and Voltaire; the power of her noose, her whip, her cauldron; the power of all the forces of the past—shows in the discomfort of the audience. They become vaguely aware of their own thin disguises, their veils: "skimpy, out-of-date voile dresses; flannel trousers; panama hats; hats wreathed in raspberry coloured net . . . seemed flimsy somehow" (110). The actors change their disguises for those of another century while La Trobe sweats to hold the audience within the circle of her creation. The bushes behind which La Trobe hides to retain her anonymity are part of nature's illusion. Lucy Swithin alone "breaking through the bushes" understands her connection with nature (112). She—"old Flimsy"—is part of the veil of Isis covering the true and the real. Cleopatra disguised herself as Isis.[21] La Trobe's artistry pulls away the disguise to reveal the woman beneath the illusion: a woman who *is* impera*trix*. To find your unacted part, your reality, is not easy. To act it out is to become vulnerable: "It's a good day, some say, the day we are stripped naked. Others, it's the end of the day" (114).

Isa too has felt the stirring of her unacted part. She wanders desolate, weighted with the burden of her superior knowledge, her artistic perceptions. The man in grey has vanished. Giles is pursuing Mrs. Manresa, and images of corruption temporarily immobilize her: commerce, ambition, violence, and the recurring "china faces glazed and hard" (115). The burden carried by the present is the apparently inescapable past. But Lucy Swithin does not believe in history. Colonel Mayhew's question, "What's history without the Army, eh?" may be answered by the future (115). Isa, the struggling writer, sees herself as a donkey: the last in the long line of a caravanseral stretching back through history, intolerably loaded. The horse is stabled; the dogs are chained. The roots of the tree of life stretch in all directions, and the branches form a ladder leading to freedom. Isa takes up the task of carrying the seeds of life, symbolised by the unripe pears, across the desert of a perilous world.

Woolf's anger at the restrictions imposed on women by the social customs of the nineteenth century is expressed in the next scene of the pageant, which Isa stoically returns to watch (113–15). The comic depiction of Victorian life is a bitterly ironic reprise of Woolf's own early life, touched, as are the previous scenes, with idiosyncratic criticisms which make "what we must remember; what we would forget" a moral lesson as much as a burden (114). An indefinable unease is evoked from the members of the audience by La Trobe's music. Some question the validity of their remembered emotion. The effort of putting that emotion into words gives a sense of struggle (extending Woolf's metaphor for the emergence of a new world) not unlike the struggle a child makes to be born—a struggle that also requires intense concentration and effort from the mother.

Mrs. Lynn Jones and Etty Springett, who share a house, "the Mount," are old earth spirits thought by the Greeks to inhabit grave mounds from which sprang new life (T 419). The cries of the street vendors of lavender, geraniums, and sweet William or pink, a type of carnation, the flower of birth, are joined in their memories by the cry of industrial progress: "any old Iron" (116). Men from "Seven Dials," the perfect order of clock time, are "Garotters", murderers who prevent women from walking on the street (116). Budge the publican is the policeman, symbolic of the era, who insists the laws of "God and Man" are obeyed. As I have suggested, Lucy Swithin, because she is Themis, defies the oppressive internal law of patriarchy represented by Budge's truncheon and the street song "Knock 'em in the Old Kent Road" (116).

Woolf proceeds to satirize the inherent hypocrisy in the highly selective concept of the white man's burden; a burden of suffering for the poor and authority for the rich, quite different from the burden that Isa has assumed as Isis, the giver of life to all. Budge the publican is in his way a life giver, for he dispenses beer and liquor at the village inn. But his name implies negative force, a refusal to move; in dialect budge is to mend a hedge, to keep barriers intact, to prevent escape. It is also a sheepskin garment, bringing to mind the divine or Dian fleece Jane Harrison described. The Greeks thought the fleece, sometimes from a black ram, would purify, would get rid of or send away pollution.[22] Budge, clothed in the black purifying garment of nineteenth-century authority, the policeman's cape, "Purity our watchword," sends the festering poor out of sight to "sweat at the mines, cough at the looms; rightly endure their lot" (119).

The scene played in front of the increasingly discomfited audience continues to question the hypocrisy beneath Victorian respectability. The setting might be taken from Chekhov's play *The Seagull,* in which the young writer Trepliov looks for new forms in writing. The scene, set in 1860, the year of Chekhov's birth, is presented, like Chekhov's play within a play, before "open space," without scenery and with "an unimpeded view."[23] As Lucy Swithin knows, the characters are only as real as their costumes make them. Mr. and Mrs. Hardcastle in Victorian dress are as believable as they are in eighteenth-century dress in Goldsmith's *She Stoops to Conquer*. By appropriating Goldsmith's names Woolf implies that the parts played are in fact conferred by superficialities such as names and costumes. The unacted part or the reality is not visible; reality or truth is conferred on the actors indirectly by their clothes because it is not *acted* until the clothes are discarded. The many guises of human beings are always, then, *disguises*.

Albert the idiot alone acts naturally as he did in the Elizabethan scene. "There was no need to dress him up" (66). He plays the hind legs of the donkey; his part is his real part, coming from his animal nature, that of the donkey. His emergence from the skin of the donkey as if reborn is a rite of passage from animal to human (T 507).[24] I have said that Albert is a scapegoat for the other characters. If Giles is the "guileless fool" he seems to be as Manresa's heroic if surly and immature knight, it is through Albert the idiot that Giles can be symbolically reborn from his animal nature. After having vicariously impersonated the hind end of the donkey, he has experienced his own lustfulness. In Albert's case the primitive part of his humanity, the common denominator others cover up, *is* his reality—which is the reason Mrs. Parker and Mrs. Springett feel uncomfortable at his vulgar behavior as Mr. Hardcastle intones a prayer (124, 125). In Giles's case his lust does not satisfy his need to be whole, that is to be human. As Mrs. Parker complains to Isa, "Oh that idiot!" Isa mentally transposes the remark to mean Giles, as she remembers his infidelities: "It made no difference; his infidelity—but hers did" (83). She must remain faithful to him for it is only through her love that he can be raised to maturity and restored to the fullness of life. To be reborn, however, he must be made to see and to speak of the truth beneath Isis's veil.[25]

Woolf's equation of Isa, the writer, with the heavily burdened donkey, suggests that the past, in the shape of Mrs. Hardcastle the well-intentioned but socially oppressed woman carried on the back of the donkey, her husband the fossil-bearing buffoon, as well as the church, may be satisfactorily ridiculed by the female writer. References to dust, skulls and Mr. Hardcastle's comic attachment to his fossil, satirize the stultifying age, dominated by rigid, Christian morality, during which Woolf grew up. Jane Harrison found the "fossilised ways of thinking" of the ancient Greeks, to whom Themis represented social order in tune with nature, very little different from the ways of thinking of Christians who look to an individual father god to approve the use of their animal or natural desires. Both primitive Greeks and Christians deny the necessity of further creation outside a given moral code (T 6, 535). The church appears appropriately small among the trees. Eleanor, her name derived from helios and Helen, meaning the sun, is not, as she tells Edgar, what she seems (121).

Jane Marcus believes the source for Eleanor in *The Years* was Margaret

Llewellyn-Davies the social reformer and Virginia Woolf's much-admired cousin. Margaret Llewellyn-Davies tried hard to improve plumbing and sanitation in the slums of England's large cities.[26] Eleanor Hardcastle, the would-be missionary in the African desert, so inhospitable to vegetation, is anxious to irrigate the sterile field of literature. She sings reluctantly, "I'd be a butterfly," Woolf's constant metaphor for women desperately seeking the freedom to be creative.[27] The butterfly represents here the world soul or collective psyche suggesting primitive thinking or the totemism Jane Harrison tells us is a stage in collective thinking, the basis of which is "group-unity, aggregation, similarity, sympathy . . . *participation*" (T 122).

Totemism, standing for the fusion of all living matter including humankind, is then in one sense a "fossil form" of belief (T 122 and n. 2). Mr. Hardcastle, a ludicrous figure "between two worlds," clasping his fossil, fumbling with it as he prays to the singular Christian god and holding it in front of him as though for protection as he "goes over the hill," calls up a response from some of the audience: "'This is too much, too much,' Mrs. Springett protested." And the hind part of the donkey, Albert the idiot, natural man, vulgarly performs his natural function (124).

The picnic hampers are unpacked on the scorched earth, signifying the place where Hades burst from the underworld in his four-horse chariot to abduct Persephone, also perhaps part of the domain of Set, the red, burning spirit of the desert whose droughts destroyed the crops in the delta of the Nile. Mrs. Hardcastle laments the loss of Mr. Beach the clergyman "(a blessed release)" (122). Beach represents the slowly dying Victorian age; "Every year one of us is missing" (122). He is also the sand at the edge of fertility and perhaps the fading cry of Matthew Arnold in "Dover Beach" for the lost "Sea of Faith."[28] Woolf alludes as well to Sylvia Beach, the original publisher of Joyce's *Ulysses*. Beach's devotion to Joyce's work and the missionary zeal with which she promoted it gave her a place in literary history from which, Woolf obliquely suggests, new readers and critics among the common people will eventually remove her.[29]

Beach's place is taken by Sibthorp, symbolizing close relations within the village (in dialect, thorp). The authority of the church is thus both diffused among the community and part of the whole. Mrs. Hardcastle's cousin is married to a Sibthorp; she would like one of her daughters to marry the clergyman, an incestuous notion closely linked among primitive people with the idea of reincarnation. Mrs. Potts, the washerwoman, the dispenser of purifying water, reports the contents of Mr. Sibthorp's luggage. All the signs of oppression by church, state and military are there: the prayer book, the academic gown, the family album, the gun, the cane and the rod. But on top of them all lies a tea cozy, embossed with a honeysuckle design. The Greeks left a meal of cooked seed in "pots" as part of the spring festival to ensure rebirth of the dead (T 275). Nectar drawn from the flower by the bee for honey is subject to an intricate process of change which makes it symbolic with rebirth and with wisdom.[30] The tea cozy linked to the tea service set out for the Age of Reason implies peace, prosperity, wisdom and renewal as a vision for the future.

Eleanor's desire to go to Africa may, on a literal level, be a desire to escape from home—a Victorian home comparable to Antigone's tomb, as Woolf well knew. Women remained at home to knit while bearded men went to rule the world. Budge leaves the stage after issuing Woolf's veiled warning against building any more patriotic towers, "Let's build: . . . shall it be a tower with our flag on top" (125). Here Woolf is reiterating the question and central concern of her essay "The Leaning Tower." "Will there be no more towers and no more classes and shall we stand, without hedges between us, on the common ground?" Woolf's prescription for survival after the unimaginable devastation of modern war is the transformation of literature: "the novel of a classless and towerless world should be a better novel than the old novel."[31]

The interval before the final act of the pageant in *Between the Acts* finds the audience struggling to bring meaning to light, struggling to bridge the gulf between a dying world and one about to be born. The motif of the year spirit bringing together the past and present, the city and the country, continues. Etty Springett finds urbane William Dodge in his birdlike outfit of green trousers and yellow spotted tie, waistcoat comfortably undone, "cheap and nasty." Old Mrs. Jones ponders the discomforts of change in the world and consoles herself with the thought, "Heaven was changeless" (127). The ticking of the machine, the gramophone, imprisons the watchers of the spectacle. They resist La Trobe's attempt to unite them in the experience of her art for, if she convinces them of the truth of her version of life, not only must they accept a changed world but they must see themselves undisguised and the qualities, good and bad, that they share.

Mrs. Manresa as goddess of the cultivated earth preserves her illusions and remains at ease for the time being. Isa, afraid of the artist's role to which she has committed herself as "the little donkey . . . crossing the desert," develops her bland poetry and a child's rhyme into a critical assessment bent on destroying La Trobe's work and her own: "Down came an Ostrich, an eagle, an executioner" (129). La Trobe, in front of her audience "felt everything they felt," the dilemma of the artist who must rouse hostility and even dislike if she is not to compromise her vision (130). It is so much easier to write a play without an audience. The spectators then are more than spectators. They become participants as in ancient ritual, but with this difference: Woolf's vision is of a play that is an art form to which all can contribute a voice, an opinion or an idea of value. This is an art of the people not of the elite, a conscious and educated art but also an art that is not barred and hedged about by a false morality enforced for the enrichment of a few, as in the Victorian age.

La Trobe's agony in the garden of Pointz Hall resembles Christ's at Gethsemane. "Blood seemed to pour from her shoes" (131). Relief comes with a shower of rain. The offering is not Christ's life to his father in heaven, but Isa's life's work to her mother the earth. "The little twist of sound could have the whole of her. On the altar of the rain-soaked earth she laid down her sacrifice . . ." (131–32). The shower of rain, natural, falling impartially on everyone, comes from the earth and is returned to it. Isis means "she who weeps."[32] Isa as artist becomes she whose tears are "all people's tears, weeping for all people" (131). The artist feels all that the audience feels because she is one of them; she is the writer of poetry not oratory.[33]

The voice that is no one's voice, "the little twist of sound" to which Isa dedicates herself, repeats the verse from "Sing a song of sixpence." This is a song of the coinlike moon and a song of money, a song of bread and of honey, symbols of wisdom and life. The song of the familiar old world of commerce and usury, of patriarchal rule, and everything in its place on the ladder of civilisation changes to a cacophony dissolving all imaginary barriers and contributed to by trees, birds, animals, actors and audience, mirrored and fragmented. The final words of the uproar are from another "simple" song, "Hark, hark the dogs do bark and the beggars . . ." (168). The barking dog, the god of speech giving tongue, heralds the beggars, those least privileged to speak, those used to depending on apple parings, crumbs and crusts from the table (108). Within the frame provided by the two nursery rhymes it is as if the inner spring of a giant clock had unwound; the clock strikes and ticks uncontrollably.

The revolutions of memory and time cease as though signalled by young Bonthorp setting down the cheval glass from the rectory. "The hands of the clock had stopped at the present moment. It was now. Ourselves" (135). The village (thorp) with all good intentions no longer has the strength to support the church, the horse (cheval) of the state with its rigid moral code (its frame) anymore than it can afford to repair the "perpetually falling steeple" encasing "rather a cracked old bell" as symbol of its creative power nor to illumine an outdated building with artificial light (22). The church is placed as is the entire company when time stops, *à cheval*, straddling two worlds, between two acts, the collective soul bared and reflected in the psyche (cheval) glass and "unable to come to any common conclusion" (135). The inadequacy of language as the sole medium of communication is at once apparent: rhyme and reason need each other. The artist must reveal the truth of trees, birds, dogs and beggars as well as kings and queens—must even, as Jane Harrison tells us, consider the bourgeois (AR 244).

In *Ancient Art and Ritual* Harrison discusses the social function of art as an expression of the emotions of a world community that she calls a "world soul" (AR 246). Virginia Woolf in *Between the Acts* reaches toward a new literature which may express the collective emotion of the world community. She is postulating a literature that cannot be reduced to a single formula or a theory but requires constant renewal of a vision to express the feelings of "people living today, in modern conditions, . . . the haste and hurry of the modern street, the whirr of motor cars and aeroplanes" (AR 237).

The anonymous voice from the bushes, in simple words without either the poet's rhyme or rhythm or the "larding, stuffing or cant" of preachers, presses home its message of communal responsibility and ironically sums up through a pattern of internal rhymes the entire theme of Woolf's *Three Guineas* (135). The process by which women can rescue the world from male destroyers becomes the symbolic artist La Trobe's creative process. From "reprobation" through "protestation," "indignation" and the desire for "immolation" emerge first "education" then "civilisation" (136), all of which seems reasonable. But, because it too is *anonymous* requiring neither place, actors, circumstances nor words, *music* is the art, more than any other, that best expresses the *emotions* of all who hear it (AR 232, 233). The task of creating a language as anonymous and as expressive as music is that to which Woolf, through La Trobe, addresses herself.

Jane Harrison quotes D.S. McColl:

> In tone and rhythm music has a notation for every kind and degree of action and passion, presenting abstract moulds of its excitement, fluctuation, suspense, crisis, appease-ment. . . . Poetry . . . can command only a few rhythms limited by the duration of a human breath and the pitch of an octave. The little effects worked out in this small compass music sweeps up and builds into vast fabrics of emotion with a dissolute freedom undreamed of in any other art. (AR 233)

Compare Woolf's lyrical description of the musical voice "speaking" from La Trobe's machine to the "scraps, orts and fragments" who are "caught and torn in the iron hands of a man-made machine, Society itself" (AR 246).

> The tune began; the first note meant a second the second a third. Then down beneath a force was born in opposition; then another. On different levels they diverged. On different levels ourselves went forward; flower gathering some on the surface; others descending to wrestle with the meaning; but all comprehending; all enlisted. The whole population of the mind's immeasurable profundity came flocking; from the unprotected, the unskinned; and dawn rose; and azure; from chaos and cacophony measure; but not the melody of surface sound alone controlled it; but also the warring battle-plumed warriors straining asunder: To part? No. Compelled from the ends of the horizon; recalled from the edge of appalling crevasses; they crashed; solved; united. (137)

Woolf illustrates in words the power music has to bring together the torn and scattered fragments of a community. In the mythological world, the industrial society is the god of the desert who ripped apart the body of Osiris, sharply dividing the parts of nature. Music, Isis the muse and the "Gods of her company" search for and reassemble all but one piece of the body. Manresa (Maneros) is reduced to tears by the intensity of the emotion she witnesses and feels.

Streatfield upon his soapbox, the traditional place of free speech and political opinions, gropes for and fails to find a verbal formula to reduce to the level of a sermon La Trobe's complex artistic presentation. "Words the defiler's . . . the impure" force the company to retreat to their separate existences, to be distinctly "Thomas or Jane." The words are the fatherly words of god's learned representative "Reverend and M.A." Streatfield, a ridiculous, irrelevant figure joined to the people of his congregation only through a common addiction to tobacco, itself a legacy from the Elizabethans whose own dramatic works were presented out-of-doors where rain and animal noises merged with the worlds of poets. The sounds of nature—"the breeze had risen; the leaves were rustling"—make the clergyman's first words inaudible. Nature is augmented by the "zoom" of the aeroplane which cuts through "the thread of his discourse." The broken thread giving him command of words comes from the cross chained to his watch, the antithesis, as we have seen, of emotional life. While contemplating the idiot (he who has no part to play, for emotion and reason are fused so that he *is* his part), Streatfield ceases to "twiddle the cross on his watchchain" and reaches into his trouser pocket seeking his natural self. He has "no further use for words" (141).

La Trobe remains invisible, anonymous; there appears to be no one in particular responsible for the entertainment. There is no satisfactory denouement, for the plot has yet to be written. "Miss La Trobe cut this knot in the centre" (69). Questions remain unanswered. What is more important, questions are asked. The fragmented conversation of the departing audience of "old cronies" (friends of long standing, made during the course of time) touches on nature, history, geography, science and religion; questions of sex, psychology, fashion, poetry, music and the social graces are set aside for later thought and discussion.

The spirit of 1939 droning through the conversation seems to be the airplane, an ambiguous symbol certainly evoking thoughts of invasion and destruction as well as escape and freedom (the Brookes in Italy may hire an aeroplane to fly home). The aeroplane can shorten and even reverse clock time, and undoubtedly the noise of its engines, one of the common voices singing out of doors, must become part of the new plot and the common language (144). Earlier in the day Isa has searched for but failed to find a word to describe the vibrations of the propeller (15). Now among the vehicles crowded together, hiding the crescent-shaped driveway, is a car, almost invisible; a monkey mascot hangs in the window.

The great earth mother and the moon goddess of the age of antiquity are together in the "gravel-strewn crescent," a firm foundation for the people and the machines of the modern age (143). The monkey-faced iconoclast of the Age of Reason looks from the window of the inescapable machine, represented by the car, as if to defy the use of those machines by his enemies, the state and the military. Thus, again, inanimate things have a voice in Woolf's language. The signs and symbols of emotion, reason and progress tell their story where words, no longer "useful" may have failed. The signs are there for all who will "see," ready to begin a new age of (the gramophone offers the alternatives with its final turns) unity or dispersity (146).

4

Epilogue

I am all that has been and is and shall be, and no mortal has ever revealed my robe.

Plutarch, Inscription on Isis monument at Sais

It is the end of the day of festival. Conflicting opinions and mixed emotions depart with the audience until "next time" (146). The members of the community have been "stripped naked" long enough to question the value of their everyday disguises (114). La Trobe the artist, goddess, spirit in hiding has forced them to think of themselves and encouraged them to talk to each other. The priests and priestesses gave their temple for her use as the director of the spectacle whence the gods, "faded, unaccomplished actions and desires" of 1939, might reveal themselves to those who long for them. Now the priestly representatives of the gods, Bart, Lucy, Giles, Isa, Manresa and Dodge, remain standing on the "ancient grass." La Trobe, the creator hides suitably in the bushes. All are ready to gather up the threads and scattered fragments of their lives. Bart, the representative of the old and dying world relinquishes Manresa, who has stirred his emotions, to his son: "Manresa turned, and Giles stepped forward" (146). The water over the lily pool, the muddy centre of creation, is opaque, obscuring future life and literature.

Lucy Swithin with her sublime faith in humankind would like to feed crumbs to the hungry fish, her totems, symbols of life to be born from the muddy waters. The great carp, seldom seen, glides to the surface for food. Carp, in dialect, is to utter or to speak. Carpo, the winter solstice, is a child of Zeus and of Themis who prophesies, in the sense of utterance, the common law of society.[1] Dodge the critic whom Lucy has healed of his emotional paralysis, prevents her from fetching the offering of a dry biscuit from Mrs. Sands, the servant of convention and tradition who cannot herself "dash off masterpieces." Lucy has given all she has to life; "She had nothing to give them—not a crumb of bread" (149). Her time, like Bart's, is past. Dodge revives her for a moment "like a girl in a garden in white among roses," another "unacted part," her natural, virginal self. Although charming to Dodge and deferential to her brother's opinions, she has courage to cling to her belief in the beauty and goodness of humankind, "the sea on which we float" (149). Her impulsive faith is tempered by Bart's reasoning: "it was always 'my brother . . . my brother' who rose from the depths of her lily pool" (150).

While Lucy Swithin contemplates feeding her fish and dreams of the future, Isa thinks of what might have been. Her animal nature, "the hot nerve wired, now lit up, now dark as the grave physical body," drives her in a passion across the lawn to where Giles stands "attached to Mrs. Manresa" (150, 151). Thwarted of the release from tension and the temporary oblivion or death a sexual union with the man in grey would bring, she "[strips] the bitter leaf" of male power from the nursery window as she sweeps imperiously past the watching Dodge. He translates from Racine's *Phèdre:* "'like Venus' . . . to her prey.'"[2] Isa, in her goddesslike fury, is Venus or Aphrodite who caused Phaedra to fall in love with her own stepson. The arrow of Eros "about to strike" may excite or repel love between Giles and Manresa. Either way Giles will know the inadequacy of mere lust and come to Isa for regeneration of his spirit.

At this point begins Virginia Woolf's profound summation of the process by which she as artist conceives, gestates and gives birth to a work of literature. The author of the pageant does not want Lucy's thanks for, as Jane Harrison tells us, the real artist cares for praise only in proportion to her certainty of success (AR 213). La Trobe has launched her play into a sea of criticism. As she crouches alone in the bushes, it seems to her "a failure"—but only momentarily (151). The inspiration for her next play is signalled by the "syllabling" starlings. Old Mrs. Chalmers creeping through the grass carrying a bunch of pinks to her dead husband's grave sets off a chain reaction *ending* in the *beginning* of the painful, lonely journey of the artist toward the production of a new work.

Woolf's symbolism is dazzlingly implicit. A chalmer, in dialect, is a room or chamber; the old lady makes her way toward the graveyard where are the chambers of the dead. The flowers she carries are a type of carnation, the flower of birth. In winter she carries holly or ivy—evergreen symbols of immortality—to fill the vessel of life, the vase on the grave mount. On her return, carrying the dead flowers she has replaced, she deliberately ignores La Trobe. The village women, who live in cottages with red geraniums, the sign for rain and the thrice-yearly ritual of plowing, make La Trobe feel an outcast. Yet they are her inspiration. She is their slave; her task in life is to speak for all the members of her audience and to make them understand the truth of their lives through her words: words spoken anonymously, for they are part of a language common to her and to them.

The rewards of a writer's life come from the ability to create another work rather than from pride in the one created. "Triumph, humiliation, ecstasy, despair" are transient emotions; joy in the work of beginning again is the only encouragement the writer has to face the "horror and terror of being alone" (153). Since the mixed critical reception of *Three Guineas,* Woolf well knew the perils of challenging the establishment, La Trobe's "village laws." La Trobe's fear of "taking something that did not properly belong to her" refers to the copying, of which Woolf was sometimes accused by critics who could not or would not see that she had her own version of the modernist vision she shared with many, including Joyce and Eliot.[3] The actress with whom La Trobe shared her bed and her purse is the writer she once was. The woman who wrote *A Room of One's Own,* although she was addressing women, wrote, as I suggested earlier, for men; the woman who wrote *Three Guineas* was politically uncompromising; the woman who wrote *Between the Acts* requires the reader to participate in the work in order to understand it fully. La Trobe, like Woolf, unites herself with her audience, yet guides them through her use of the language common to them all.

La Trobe needs intoxicating drink since the estrangement from her previous, more artificial, nonparticipatory self. She can no longer invent a novel or a play without inspiration from the common people. Dionysos is the god of the people; his drink, whether beer, wine or the whiskey and soda Bart prescribes, will send coarse words to the depths of her mind like "maggots through the waters" to the carp in the lily pool (147).

La Trobe strides across the lawn to find her inspiration. The landscape with its characteristic view begins to fade with the twilight; green waters seem to rise from the earth to sweep La Trobe on her quest "away from the shore" (153). She takes her case of gramophone records to the kitchen of the private house before she walks to the public house. The case contains the songs and dances that are essential ingredients for the brew in her cauldron of regeneration. She fumbles for the latch of the iron gate and thrusts the suitcase through the small aperture of the scullery window: sexual images perfectly in keeping with the conception of the new work about to germinate. In the hospitable, smoke-filled atmosphere of the village pub, "Bossy," accepting her cow's name, sits and drinks, "arms akimbo," before a "crude glass painting" of a cow and one of a cock and a hen (153).

The posture is a curious one for drinking, or even for thinking until we consider Harrison's description of an Egyptian bas relief showing the outspread wings of Isis, mother and life, sheltering Osiris, all of nature, at his resurrection (AR 18). The crudity of the execution and subject matter of the public house paintings contrasts with the artistry of the pictures of the long lady and the aristocratic man in the dining room of Pointz Hall. But beer intoxicates as well as champagne; barnyard life cannot be separated from nature. La Trobe, Bossy, is accompanied by her symbols. The cheap clock ticks to remind us that time is no longer suspended. The cow is not bellowing from the meadow nor coughing in the garden; like the butler's watch on the landing of Pointz Hall she is encased in glass. Her work is done. She peacefully reflects the creative process of the anonymous artist giving birth to words that may save the world from destruction.

The most obvious inference and I think Woolf's ironic intention is comparison with the birth of Christ—supposedly in a stable among farmyard animals.

Christ, the Word of God made flesh, was born to give humanity a second chance to attain paradise. His word was the word of his father, 2000 years ago a new patriarchal law of love. In 1939, considering the history of ecclesiastical violence, that law retains very little meaning. La Trobe, the living metaphor, incubates words without meaning. The words are the nucleus of a universal language informed by reason, emotion and all knowledge and can only be intelligible when heard by those from whom they came—the entire population of the natural world.

The vision is grandiose, implying genius or even perfection. The representatives of the old and new worlds and the participants in the work in process come together for the last meal of the day. Isa has renounced sterility in the form of speechless and now invisible Rupert Haines and conformity in the form of William Dodge, her "semblable," the lip reader who contemplates the words of others and hesitates to speak his own thoughts. She has already made her decision to assume the burden of artistic integrity by offering herself as sacrifice on the altar of her mother the earth. She refuses Giles's offer of a banana, "its sheaf sliced in four, exposing a white cone." He extinguishes his lighted match. "Out it went with a little fizz in the raspberry juice" (155). In Plutarch's legend Isis never finds the phallus to complete the body of Osiris she reassembles from the scattered pieces gathered on her voyage. Instead she makes and consecrates an image of the phallus, by which she conceives and bears a lame child.[4] Isa refuses the ludicrous banana image for she does not intend to give birth to a deformed or unhealthy child. Woolf has told us how unlikely it is that a work of genius will emerge from the writer's mind "whole and entire."[5]

On the way from the dining room to "the big room with the windows open to the garden" where the novel begins and ends, Lucy stops for a "voyage into the picture" painted by Canaletto or a contemporary, appearing afterward with her black, sequinned shawl and reflective glasses, timeless as the waning moon and tragic as Isis returning from the sorrowing search in her boat for the dead Osiris (155). Isis is frequently represented as black or wearing a black cloak.[6] Lucy perceives a veiled woman or perhaps a man, an anonymous figure in the hood of the Venetian gondola, reminding us that faithful Isis has not abandoned her search. The boat carrying the human race rides on a sea of faith in its own worth, "the sea on which we float. Mostly impervious, but surely every boat sometimes leaks?" (149) Doubts may creep in, but the boat will carry those determined as Lucy is to unite the disparate. Osiris and Dionysos (they are interchangeable) must be transplanted to the city, as Peisistratos the benevolent tyrant of ancient Greece understood. The modern artist can and must look for inspiration in the busy streets (or waterways) of commerce.

Everyday routine occupations disturb and interrupt the imaginative process. Isa sews and attends to her household bills. Giles and Bart read the newspaper; Giles studies business documents. Mrs. Sands makes up the fire, and Candish stokes the boiler. Lucy knits. Time passes: "the second hand jerked on" (156). In the circle of the reading lamp, Isa has an extraordinary perception of Bart, Giles and Lucy as industrious insects rolling pebbles of sunbaked earth in front of them. "Bartholomew, Giles and Lucy polished and nibbled and broke off crumbs" (157). They are like writers revising their works, sampling and selecting words. Crumb again is Woolf's metaphor for word. The scarab beetle, venerated in ancient Egypt and connected with Osiris as sun god, rolls its egg in a ball of dirt in front of itself.[7] Isa's observation implies that literature, if it is truly common ground, may be nourished to new growth by the warmth and brilliance of the sun's rays.

"The clock ticked." The day is over. Lucy stands silent. As Themis she must pass her responsibility for unification on through Isa to the babies who sleep in a simulated death or rite of passage beneath paper roses left over from the coronation two years before. Light has faded from the garden; "roses had withdrawn for the night" (157). The paper roses, inferior but adequate temporary substitutes for Isis's symbols of love, will protect the children until morning. Coronation is the original form of carnation and of course is another rite of passage from one kind of life to another of greater responsibility.

Bartholomew adds his approval of the paper roses to Lucy's words. He is "leafless, spectral and his chair monumental." He is Osiris in his coffin, grown into the trunk of a tree from which the branches have been lopped. He goes to rest, accompanied by his dog who is also his embalmer.[8] Absorbed in her history book, Lucy reads to the end of the chapter where "Man raised great stones." She continues to affirm her faith in the future. The Egyptian sun god's best-known totem was the obelisk, the raised stone needle and image of a ray of sunlight. It is also Bart's, Lucy's and Giles's totem and the symbol of the phallus desired by Isa. Lucy has discharged her responsibility; her chapter is over, and she herself becomes part of history as she tiptoes from the room into the past.

Giles and Isa, the inheritors, set aside their mundane affairs: she drops her sewing, and he crumples the newspaper. The stage is dark and empty. The final scene in which Woolf leaves Giles and Isa in darkness does not evoke the pessimism of Matthew Arnold's "darkling plain" of the nineteenth century, nor the horror of Conrad's heart of darkness which T.S. Eliot used as an epigraph for the wasteland of the twentieth century.[9] The quarrel at the end of a day of suspicion, frustration and very little joy, vicious and cruel as it may be, will release powerful, undisguised feelings and end in a sexual embrace.

The huge, symbolic, seated figures, reminiscent of Egyptian temple carvings, lose their humanity and become the primitive gods that are really nothing more than conceptions of the human mind. In the end they are created, in Miss La Trobe's imagination, "two scarcely perceptible figures" (154). The two figures emerging through smoke and haze are Isa and Giles, Isis and Osiris, Aphrodite and Dionysos—all our "unaccomplished actions and desires" revealed to us by the artist. The words they speak are Virginia Woolf's, Miss La Trobe's and our own. Because all consciousness is in the present we cannot hear those words, for as soon as they are spoken they are past. On the other hand, consciousness is an anticipation of the future, so we can never cease, as the clock ticks away, to look forward to speaking them and to hearing them. Woolf could not tell us what we ourselves will say. What she did was to give us an imaginative fictional model of an interval in time, in a world held within the circle of its own single revolution, to reflect on all things past, and the encouragement to continue to read and speak and to write to each other of the truths we may perceive beneath the veil of Isis.

Afterword

Act Two

*The transaction between a writer and the spirit of the age is one of
infinite delicacy, and upon a nice arrangement between the two the
whole fortune of his works depend.*

Virginia Woolf, *Orlando*

"How difficult to come to any conclusion!" (120). But how important to
communicate. When the audience "turned to one another and began to talk," Miss
La Trobe, hiding behind her tree, was ready, script in hand, to record and make
whole and give a common meaning to the "scraps, and fragments" of their
conversation (90). Having in a sense defied the "spirit in hiding" by taking apart
the text of *Between the Acts* in order to understand more of Virginia Woolf's
meaning than seemed at first apparent, I now hesitate to offer any "servitude to the
summing up," making words "impure" and meaningless, and try to show instead
that my reading of the text contributes to unity (138).

The thread of communication between Woolf and those who continue her
depends for its delicate strength on whatever "arrangement" those imbued with the
spirit of a new age, modern readers and writers, can make with a writer whose
work now seems to show her dissatisfaction with a language whose words have so
many meanings and are open to so many interpretations that their usefulness in the
communication of ideas is in question.

Virginia Woolf's view of the world was, as I have said, her version of the
modernist vision shared by many of her contemporaries. For example, in "Burnt
Norton," the first poem of *Four Quartets,* T.S. Eliot described the "still point of
the turning world," a passive moment transcending time and an image startlingly
similar to Woolf's Pointz Hall, itself suspended in time.[1] "East Coker," a poem
Woolf describes as "didactic" is, in part, Eliot's exploration of the inadequacies of
a language difficult to "get the better of" and no longer useful to express the
"undisciplined squads of emotion" that plague the poet as he grows older.[2] Eliot
believes that, through the divine and human nature he shares with God, his

beginning and his end are one and the same—a perspective somewhat different from Jane Harrison's view that if Alpha and Omega are one and the same, like the symbolic bird and fish and Woolf's "monstrous inversion," the snake and the toad, there can be no union, no new birth, no continuance.

Jane Harrison, a great and humble scholar, confesses, in her preface to the second edition of Themis (1926), to an "intemperate antipathy" to the Olympians: intemperate because she, a disciple of Nietzsche, failed to consider his thesis that the irrational passions of Dionysos must fuse with the reason, measure and logic of Apollo to take care of human need and, one may assume, to make possible the birth of great literature and art: in Nietzsche's terms, tragedy (T viii). The question of words and their usefulness in the conveyance of meaning and truth is a complex one that has been addressed by many others since Nietzsche became known for his anagrams and plays on words as well as his theories on Greek tragedy. Nineteenth-century deconstructionist Ferdinand de Saussure, whom Woolf may have read although I have found no direct evidence, cites the anagram as an "indeterminable multiplicity. . .which undoes all codes."[3] This certainly shakes up but does not destroy the notion of definition, for it is definition itself. Yet it seems to fit with Woolf's "thousand possibilities" and the open-ended text of *Between the Acts.*

Among an influential group of contemporary French feminists who oppose and resist masculinist thinking, Hélène de Cixous considers that woman's writing, if it is an authentic voice, must be formed (or formless) as a reflection of her sexuality: a sexuality diffused (unlike men's sexuality which is centralized, not surprisingly, around the penis) and speaking "the language of a thousand tongues which knows neither enclosure nor death."[4] This all sounds appealing but takes no account of a social context which, as Ann Rosalind Jones points out, is the source of the notion of female sexuality as the polar opposite to male sexuality: a sexuality associated, for men at least, with convenient, useful and nonthreatening feminine qualities such as nurturance, gentleness and empathy.

Virginia Woolf knew that sexual identity does not form in isolation, and her image of the rock in the deep lake on which the female writer's imagination may founder is well known.[5] She accepted Harrison's view that fusion is needed for harmony, but she also considered that the diffusion of female wisdom in the person of Themis, the unifier and "supreme social fact" was the only chance for the world to write a "new plot" undetermined, and this is the point, by any previous themistes.

The question Woolf posed in her 1937 talk "Craftsmanship," "How can we combine words in new orders to that they survive, so that they create beauty, so that they tell the truth?" may be answered in the same words as the question Mrs. Manresa poses in *Between the Acts,* "Is it permitted Mrs. Swithin?"[6] Manresa needs no reply from Lucy for they are "con/spirators." Being women they literally breathe together, infused with the collective spirit or psyche. (34) Manresa's question and the answer, "Yes, everything can be said in this house," echo and restate Nietzsche's dictum, "Nothing is true, everything is permitted" (35).[7] In Pointz Hall, the house of language with many rooms, Woolf's surface meanings are clear, valid and acceptable but do not tell all the truth. Every specific truth can lie, but if "everything can be said" then social determinants no longer confine words and meanings. Truth transcends definition as it becomes limitless, and we are free to search for what is real.

If one woman told the truth about her life "the world would split open," American poet Muriel Ruykeser tells us in a powerful bodily image expressing the painful struggle of the woman artist in the process of creation.[8] In *Between the Acts* Virginia Woolf anticipates Ruykeser and, I think, de Cixous and other feminist writers seeking to cast off the hair-thin ties, the tangles of dirty duckweed, the psychosocial bonds and gags of centuries of suppression of women's authentic voices. Mrs. Manresa defies convention and takes off her stays. "She had given up dealing with her figure and thus gained freedom" is Woolf's way of saying that women can be truthful if they cast off conformity in favour of freely expressed pleasure in their sexuality. "Pleasure's what they want"; Pleasure, the daughter of Psyche and Cupid, the child of spiritual and erotic love, was conceived only after heroic persistence on the part of her mother (35).[9]

Isa understands that Manresa's behaviour is genuine. Contemporary French novelist Christiane Rochefort, quoted by Jones, recognises how difficult it is for a woman writer to say anything not socially determined—"It is not easy to be genuine"—or to find your "unacted part."[10] When Lucy Swithin revives at the sight of William Dodge, "like a girl in a garden in white among roses. . .an unacted part," she has overcome the limitations of truth and time in a transcendent moment which contrasts with Eliot's restricted vision in "Burnt Norton" (149). He sees only the memory of the "door we never opened / Into the rose garden."[11] Woolf takes us further, opens doors as Lucy Swithin opens them, "as if she did not know what she would find" (87), and continues her quest for the language of beauty and truth, of unity and community and their extension, survival.

The survival of the questing hero may be threatened on the journey. Psyche had to outwit killer sheep and the guard dog of the underworld. Woolf's irony challenges the reader who would rest satisfied, who fails to understand that "large oil paintings of fabulous fleshy monsters complete from top to toe" created by male writers "Hugh Walpole, Wells, etc. etc. etc." are forever framed, barred and, unlike La Trobe's scullery window with its tiny aperture, are closed to life or sterile (153). Woolf's comments about monsters, made in a 1922 letter to a young writer who sought her advice, followed her thoughts about the difficulties of capturing in art the elusive human spirit: "The human soul. . .orientates itself afresh every now and then. It is doing so now. No one can see it whole, therefore. The best of us catch a glimpse of a nose, a shoulder, something turning away, always in movement."[12]

Kinetic Lucy Swithin, seldom still, remembers her mother saying "Never play. . .on people's names" (28). Deliberately, as though in response, Woolf applies in her text the power of music to words. She plays variations on a leitmotif, each variation adding dimension to the meaning for the reader who in turn must add meaning in what may be "a very different world" (11). Woolf told us "we have to allow the sunken meanings to remain sunken, suggested not stated; lapsing and flowing into each other like reeds on the bed of a river." To read, we must employ "the imagination, the memory, the eye and the ear."[13] The language of survival then is not a language of separation where each word proclaims one factual meaning. Woolf prophesied, with some scorn, that a language of signs—stars, arrows and so forth—will eventually suffice to communicate simple facts. Truth can come from the unstated, the hidden, the "slant" in a writer's text. And the "transaction" readers of every age can make with the writer is to allow their emotion, reason and familiarity with language to sink into the fertile mud of the mind in combination with the writer's words: a communal act to evoke unique meanings. We can only describe what we have access to. Yet we cannot deny the perceptions of others. Although we may argue with them.

The assembly to which Woolf, through Lucy as Themis and through La Trobe as artist in hiding, has called the populace of the novel, the readers of the text and—if we can be clear—the writer and the readers of this criticism, is the moment in time or the moment of consciousness at which we meet as a community to find a meaning and to come to a "common conclusion." Out of the desire to reach a "common conclusion" comes the argument; from the argument comes the unity that conceives another work of poetry, fiction or criticism (135). If future life depends on re/creation through conflict, as the ending of *Between the Acts* suggests, we as readers, speakers and writers must find a place in the community to participate in the creative conflict. Finding that place is the political reality that Woolf understood and that she left us to deal with.

Virginia Woolf's invention of "the common reader" suggests a community from which no one need be excluded. However, critics Barbara Currier Bell and Carol Ohmann point out that to Woolf the existence of that community was never a foregone conclusion.[14] The struggle to find equality, and freedom to write or to speak is as daunting as the umpteenth revision of a book. Woolf's *Orlando* found equality—she had neither to fight against nor to submit to the demands of her age. And having found her place in the world, "She wrote. She wrote. She wrote."[15]

Our fight is against the enemy common to us and to those before us on the literary continuum: Voltaire's *l'infâme*, Jane Harrison's archpatriarchal bourgeois, Virginia Woolf's educated men.[16] We wage war with a common weapon: language constantly renewed and revitalized by the desire to find a place for all its forms and variation. The complicated, tiring work of creation continues because, like La Trobe's audience in *Between the Acts*, we are together "(stooping, peering, fumbling). . . .And there is joy, sweet joy in company"

(143). Any visions of "glory," the revelations of truth transcending the "daily drop of the daily bill" are necessarily momentary, "Or every man be blind."[17]

Virginia Woolf had a "persistent vision" of a mountain top from which she looked to the future. That mountain peak was to be the starting point of her next book, "a supported on fact book."[18] Those facts would reflect the doings, in the present, of the ever-moving, ever-generating, never-completed world: Alpha not Omega. Although Woolf will not write her book, as long as we who continue her carry on with our work, the second act of the drama we are making together will never be played out. For as we speak, write, or read, each word becomes part of the first act, the past. And our words will not be criticised until the anticipated but unattainable future.

Notes

Introduction

1. Adrienne Rich, *On Lies, Secrets and Silence* (New York: W.W. Norton, 1979), p. 37.

2. Virginia Woolf, *The Sickle Side of the Moon,* Vol. V of *The Letters of Virginia Woolf, 1932–1935,* ed. Nigel Nicolson and Joanne Trautmann (London: Chatto and Windus, 1982), p. 195.

3. Herbert Marder, *Feminism and Art: A Study of Virginia Woolf* (Chicago: University of Chicago Press, 1968), p. 175.

4. Madeline Moore, "Virginia Woolf's *The Years* and Years of Adverse Male Reviewers," *Women's Studies,* 4 (1977), 259.

5. Sandra M. Gilbert and Susan Gubar, *The Madwoman in the Attic* (New Haven: Yale University Press, 1979), p. 73.

6. Virginia Woolf, *To the Lighthouse* (London: Harvest, 1978), p. 79.

7. Berenice A. Carroll, "To Crush Him in Our Own Country: The Political Thought of Virginia Woolf," *Feminist Studies,* 4, No. 4 (1978), 105.

8. Virginia Woolf, "Craftsmanship," *Collected Essays* (New York: Harcourt, Brace & World, 1967), II, p. 251.

9. Carroll, p. 105.

10. Woolf, *Letters,* V, p. 195.

11. Virginia Woolf, *A Room of One's Own* (New York: Panther, 1977), p. 83.

12. Virginia Woolf, *Three Guineas* (Middlesex: Penguin, 1977), p. 94, and note p. 190.

13. Virginia Woolf, "The Leaning Tower," *Collected Essays,* II, pp. 176–78.

14. Virginia Woolf, *Leave the Letters Till We're Dead,* Vol. VI of *The Letters of Virginia Woolf, 1936–1941* (1980), p. 468.

15. Woolf, "The Leaning Tower," p. 179.

16. W.H. Mellers, "Scrutiny," in *Virginia Woolf: The Critical Heritage,* ed. Robin Majumbar and Allen McLaurin (London: Routledge and Kegan Paul, 1975), p. 395.

17. Virginia Woolf, *The Diary of Virginia Woolf 1925–1930,* Vol. III, ed. Anne Olivier Bell and Andrew McNeillie (New York: Harcourt Brace Jovanovich, 1981), p. 193. E.M. Forster in *Recollections of Virginia Woolf,* ed. Joan Russell Noble (Middlesex: Penguin, 1972), p. 239.

18. Leon Edel, *Bloomsbury: A House of Lions* (New York: Lippincott, 1979), p. 228.

19. Virginia Woolf, *The Diary of Virginia Woolf 1920–1924,* Vol. II (1980), p. 65.

20. Woolf, *The Diary,* II, p. 79.

21. Virginia Woolf, *A Change of Perspective,* Vol. III of *The Letters of Virginia Woolf, 1923–1928* (1980), p. 458.

22. T.S. Eliot, "The Hollow Men," *The Complete Poems and Plays 1909–1950* (New York: Harcourt, Brace & World, 1958), p. 58. Matthew Arnold, "Dover Beach," *Selected Poems,* ed. E.K. Brown (New York: Appleton-Century-Crofts, 1951), p. 54.

23. Woolf, *The Diary,* II, pp. 67, 68, 125.

24. Woolf, *The Question of Things Happening,* Vol. II of *The Letters of Virginia Woolf, 1912–1922* (1980), p. 231 and note.

25. Woolf, *The Diary,* II, pp. 200, 203.

26. Virginia Woolf, *Between the Acts* (New York: Panther, 1978), p. 156. All further references in the text are to page numbers in this edition.

27. Woolf, *A Room of One's Own,* pp. 93–95.

28. All dictionary definitions are from *The Compact Edition of the Oxford English Dictionary,* 1981.

29. Woolf, *A Room of One's Own,* p. 94.

30. Josephine Donovan, "Afterword: Critical Re-vision," *Feminist Literary Criticism: Explorations in Theory,* ed. Josephine Donovan (Lexington: University Press of Kentucky, 1975). See pp. 75–76 for a brief discussion of the "prophetic" mode of criticism and of Marcuse and the possible synthesis of Logos and Eros: in Marcuse's terms, two "negative modes."

31. Virginia Woolf, Introduction, *Mrs. Dalloway* (New York: Modern Library, 1928), p. viii.

Chapter 1

1. Woolf, *A Room of One's Own,* p. 18. See also Jane Ellen Harrison, *Themis: A Study of the Social Origins of Greek Religion* (London: Merlin, 1963), p. 323: "the new year began in academic fashion in the autumn or early winter."

2. Jane Ellen Harrison, *Ancient Art and Ritual* (New York: Greenwood Press, 1969), p. 124. All references in the text are to page numbers in this edition, prefaced by AR.

3. Jane Ellen Harrison, *Prolegomena to the Study of Greek Religion* (New York: Meridian, 1960), p. 164.

4. Harrison, *Themis,* p. 185. All references in the text are to page numbers in this edition, prefaced by T.

5. Jane Marcus, "Pargeting 'The Pargiters': Notes of an Apprentice Plasterer," *Bulletin of the New York Public Library,* 80 (1976–77), 420.

6. Harrison, *Prolegomena,* p. 164.

7. Jane Marcus, "Some Sources for *Between the Acts,*" *Virginia Woolf Miscellany,* Winter 1977, and Judy Little, "Festive Comedy in Woolf's *Between the Acts,*" *Women and Literature,* 5, No. 1 (1977), 26–37.

8. Rousseau, quoted in John Berger, "Why Look at Animals?" *About Looking* (New York: Pantheon, 1980), p. 5.

9. Edel, p. 227.

10. Woolf, *Three Guineas,* p. 62.

11. Woolf, *Letters,* VI, p. 453. Although Virginia Woolf made light of Lady Oxford's gift, she mentioned it in letters to Angelica Bell (December 23, 1940), Ethel Smythe (December 24, 1940), Vita Sackville-West (December 26, 1940), Sybil Colefax (January 4, 1941), and Mary Hutchinson (February 10, 1941). Note that Leonard Woolf took with him to Ceylon in 1905 a wooden case containing the complete works of Voltaire in 70 volumes. When he returned in 1911, shortly before marrying Virginia, he left them behind. See George Spater and Ian Parsons, *A Marriage of True Minds* (New York: Harcourt Brace Jovanovich, 1977), pp. 51, 56.

12. Woolf, *A Room of One's Own,* p. 96.

13. Stuart Curran, ed., *Le Bossu and Voltaire on the Epic* (Gainesville: Scholars Facsimiles and Reprints, 1970), p. xii.

14. Jane Marcus has convinced us that Woolf derived the Pargiter family name in *The Years* from the dialect word "parget," meaning "to plaster." Boss, meaning the plasterer's tray, clearly signifies Woolf's view of the artist as a unifier. See Marcus, "Pargeting 'The Pargeters,' " p. 416.

15. J. Cuthbert Hadden, *The Operas of Wagner* (London: T.C. and E.C. Jack, 1911), p. 237.

16. Werner J. Deiman, "History Pattern and Continuity in Virginia Woolf," *Virginia Woolf,* ed. Thomas S.W. Lewis (New York: McGraw-Hill 1975), p. 140.

17. Woolf, Introduction to *Mrs. Dalloway,* p. vii.

18. Woolf, Introduction to *Mrs. Dalloway,* p. vi.

Chapter 2

1. M. Esther Harding, *Woman's Mysteries Ancient and Modern* (New York: Harper Colophon, 1971), pp. 171–73.

2. Berger, p. 6.

3. Harding, p. 140.

4. I am indebted to Carolyn G. Heilbrun for drawing my attention to the question inherent in Isa.

5. William Shakespeare, *As You Like It,* ed. T.J.B. Spencer (Middlesex: Penguin, 1968), I, iii, 73.

6. Robert Graves, *The Greek Myths* (Middlesex: Penguin, 1973), I, 126.

7. Harding, p. 98.

8. Lord Macaulay, "The Battle of Naseby," *Palgrave's Golden Treasury,* ed. Francis Turner Palgrave (London: Oxford University Press, 1926), p. 324. See Virginia Woolf, *Moments of Being,* ed. Jeanne Schulkind (London: Triad/Panther, 1978), p. 108 for her reference to a walk in Kensington Gardens, taking the *Golden Treasury* to read. I have a leather-bound copy of this then-popular anthology given by my father to my mother to mark their engagement in 1928. My mother occasionally recited "The Battle of Naseby" in its entirety.

9. Rupert Brooke, *The Collected Poems of Rupert Brooke: With a Memoir,* ed. E. Marsh (London: Sidgewick and Jackson, 1925), p. cliii.

10. Thomas Bulfinch, *The Age of Chivalry*, Vol. I of *Bulfinch's Mythology* (New York: Mentor, 1962), p. 382.

11. Richard Ellmann, "*Ulysses:* A Short History," Afterword to James Joyce, *Ulysses* (London: Penguin, 1979), p. 707.

12. Graves, I, p. 126.

13. Graves, I, p. 126.

14. Mrs. Haines's ancestral home is near the village of Liskeard (7). I suggest Liskeard is an anagram of Dark Isle which refers to Crete, in particular to Palaikastro where the hymn to Zeus, on which Jane Harrison bases her thesis of the matrilinear structure of Greek religion, was discovered. The letters of the *sound* of Liskeard—phonetically Liskar—are contained in the word Palaikastro. See Harrison's *Themis*, ch. 1, pp. 1–6.

15. Harrison, *Prolegomena*, p. 281.

16. Harding, p. 174.

17. Matthew Arnold, "Sohrab and Rustum," *Selected Poems*, ll. 230, 659, 841, 842, 857–59, pp. 21–35.

18. Aristophanes, "Lysistrata," trans. Donald Sutherland, *Comedy: A Critical Anthology*, ed. Robert W. Corrigan (Boston: Houghton Mifflin, 1971), cf. "Chorus of old men," pp. 12, 13. T.S. Eliot, "The Hollow Men," *The Complete Poems and Plays*, p. 56.

19. Robert Graves, *The White Goddess* (New York: Farrar, Straus and Giroux, 1980), pp. 196–97. In mythology the little finger has oracular and divinatory significance as the finger most easily put into one's ear. The usual ring finger, the fourth, is associated with Apollo.

20. Arnold, "Sohrab and Rustum," l. 381, p. 24.

21. "Bartholomew," *Catholic Encyclopaedia*, The Family Rosary Edition of the Holy Bible, ed. Rev. John P. O'Connell (Chicago: The Catholic Press, 1952), p. 26.

22. Virginia Woolf, *The Diary of Virginia Woolf 1931–1935*, Vol. IV (1982), p. 324.

23. Harding, pp. 181–83.

24. Woolf, *A Writer's Diary*, ed. Leonard Woolf (London: Triad/Panther, 1979), pp. 311–12. Virginia describes Leonard's criticism of her biography of Roger Fry as "being pecked by a very hard, strong, beak." See also Woolf, *To the Lighthouse*, p. 58, "the fatal sterility of the male plunged itself, like a beak of brass, barren and bare."

25. Edward Tripp, *The Meridian Handbook of Classical Mythology* (New York: New American Library, 1970), p. 596.

26. Woolf, *Three Guineas*, p. 190, n. 40.

27. See Woolf, *The Diary*, II, p. 123. In a review of the Hogarth Press publication, Gorky's *The Notebooks of Tchekhov*, Middleton Murray criticised "'the tendency to approach an author by the backstairs'" in this case the publication of manuscripts not authorised for publication by the writer.

28. Robert Briffault, *The Mothers* (1927), abridged Gordon Rattray Taylor (New York: Atheneum, 1977), p. 375.

29. Harding, p. 94.

30. Briffault, p. 58.

31. Briffault, p. 375.

32. Harding, p. 161.

33. Algernon Swinburne, "Itylus," *Collected Poetical Works,* I (London: Wm. Heinemann, 1924), p. 54.

34. Eliot, "The Waste Land," *The Complete Poems and Plays,* 1. 18, p. 37.

35. Alban Butler, *The Lives of the Saints* (New York: P.J. Kenedy and Sons, 1963), III, p. 108, and IV, p. 548.

36. Woolf, "The Leaning Tower," p. 179.

37. Woolf, *A Room of One's Own,* pp. 46–47.

38. Harding, p. 128.

39. Virginia Woolf, quoted in Quentin Bell, *Virginia Woolf: A Biography* (London: Triad/Paladin, 1976), I, *1892–1912,* p. 138: "As for writing. . .I. . .achieve in the end, some kind of whole made of shivering fragments; to me this seems the natural process; the flight of the mind."

40. J.E. Cirlot, *A Dictionary of Symbols,* trans. Jack Sage (New York: Routledge and Kegan Paul, 1974), pp. 8, 9.

41. Virginia Woolf, Introduction to *Mrs. Dalloway,* p. v.

42. Voltaire, *Candide,* trans. John Butt (Middlesex: Penguin, 1982), p. 106.

43. Voltaire, p. 20.

44. Voltaire, p. 144.

45. Harrison, *Prolegomena,* p. 275.

46. William Wordsworth, "Lines Composed a Few Miles above Tintern Abbey," *Selected Poems,* ed. Walford Davies (London: J.M. Dent, 1975), 11. 96, 133–34, 118, 119, pp. 39–42.

47. Harrison, *Prolegomena,* pp. 274–75.

48. Harding, p. 136. Soma, wine of the gods and brewed from the moon tree, has an earthly counterpart, an intoxicating drink.

49. Harding, p. 129.

50. Woolf, *A Room of One's Own,* pp. 50, 51.

51. Harding, p. 174.

52. Woolf, *A Writer's Diary,* p. 340

53. Woolf, *Three Guineas,* p. 82 and Woolf, *Letters,* VI, pp. 166, 167. On September 2, 1937, Virginia Woolf wrote to Victoria Ocampo who had lectured on her works in Brazil, "I suspect you are one of the people. . .who can make a lecture exciting. I would rather sit in a cellar or watch spiders than listen to an Englishman lecturing."

54. R.R. Palmer and Joel Colton, *A History of the Modern World* (New York: Alfred A. Knopf, 1971), p. 94.

55. Harrison, *Prolegomena,* p. 273.

56. Woolf, *The Diary*, IV, p. 338. Virginia Woolf's entry for September 4, 1935 recorded that she and Leonard had watched a snake eat a toad in their garden. "We saw a snake eat a toad: it had half the toad in, half out; gave a suck now and then. The toad slowly disappearing. L. poked its tail; the snake was sick of the crushed toad, and I dreamt of men committing suicide and cd. see the body shooting through the water."

57. Virginia Woolf met the poet and novelist Sylvia Townsend Warner (1893–1978) in 1925 and approved of her. "Indeed she has some merit—enough to make me spend 2/6 on her I think." (*The Diary*, III, p. 26. Warner's novel *The True Heart* (1928) retells in disguised form the tale of Cupid and Psyche from Apuleius. Warner's clues to the identities of her characters lay in their names. She revealed her ingenious game shortly before she died in 1978. "These disguises were so efficient that no reviewer saw what I was up to." She added, as if to prove the worth of feminist criticism, "Only my mother recognised the basis of the story." Woolf may have seen through the disguise and adapted Warner's method for her own purposes in *Between the Acts*. Isa's remark about William Dodge, "Always some cold eye crawled over the surface like a winter bluebottle!" (128) is strikingly similar to that of Warner's Sukey (Psyche): "She could not help feeling their eyes crawling over her like bluebottles." See Warner, *The True Heart* (London: Virago, 1978), p. 113 and preface.

58. George Gordon, Lord Byron, "Inscription on the Monument of a Newfoundland Dog," *The Complete Poetical Works* (Boston: Houghton Mifflin, 1933), p. 154, and Byron, "Inscription on the Monument of a Newfoundland Dog," *Bartlett's Familiar Quotations*, ed. John Bartlett (Boston: Little, Brown and Company, 1968), p. 554.

59. Woolf, "The Leaning Tower," pp. 178, 179.

60. Butler, III, p. 457.

61. Byron, "Don Juan," *The Complete Poetical Works*, Canto the Ninth, Stanza xxxii, l. 3. The stanza continues, "lately there have been no rents at all/And 'gentlemen' are in a piteous plight./And 'farmers' can't raise Ceres from her fall;/She fell with Buonaparte."

62. Larousse, *World Mythology*, ed. Pierre Grimal (New York: Excalibur, 1981), p. 32.

63. Harding, p. 161.

64. Harrison, *Prolegomena*, pp. 74–75.

65. Harding, p. 161.

66. Woolf, *A Writer's Diary*, p. 184.

67. Woolf, "The Leaning Tower," p. 181.

68. J[ohn] W. O[sborne] "William Cobbett" *Encyclopaedia Britannica: Macropaedia* (1974 ed.), IV, p. 809.

69. E.P. Thompson, *The Making of the English Working Class* (Harmondsworth: Pelican, 1963), p. 782.

70. Osborne, p. 810.

71. Thompson, p. 829. Woolf, *Letters*, IV, p. 168. Virginia Woolf reviewed *The Complete Works of William Hazlitt* for the *New York Herald Tribune*, September 7, 1930.

72. Voltaire, pp. 83–84.

73. Judy Little, "Festive Comedy in Woolf's *Between the Acts*," *Women and Literature*, 5 (1977), 31–32.

Chapter 3

1. Bell, I, p. 51. and II, *1912–1941*, p. 47.

2. Brenda Silver, "Virginia Woolf and the Concept of Community: The Elizabethan Playhouse," *Women's Studies*, 2–3 (1977), 293.

3. Woolf, "Notes on an Elizabethan Play," *The Common Reader* (New York: Harvest, 1953), p. 56.

4. Harding, pp. 172, 174–75.

5. William Shakespeare, *King Lear*, ed. Alfred Harbage (New York: Pelican, 1979), IV, vii, 63, p. 146.

6. Shakespeare, *Lear*, I, iv, 174–76, p. 57.

7. Shakespeare, *Lear*, IV, i, 61, 62, p. 120.

8. Larousse, pp. 182, 183 and Tripp, p. 515.

9. Thomas Bulfinch, *Bulfinch's Mythology* (New York: Mentor, 1962), I, p. 51.

10. Tripp, p. 66.

11. Larousse, p. 26 and Briffault, p. 301.

12. Larousse, p. 26.

13. François Rabelais, *Gargantua and Pantagruel bk. III Rabelais the Reader*, Ch. 31, in Bartlett, p. 181. The actual quotation is "This flea which I have in mine ear."

14. John Lemprière, *Lemprière's Classical Dictionary of Proper Names in Ancient Authors* (London: Routledge and Kegan Paul, 1958) and Larousse, p. 131.

15. Larousse, p. 33.

16. Mary Daly, *Gyn/Ecology* (Boston: Beacon, 1978), pp. 82, 194.

17. Woolf, *A Writer's Diary*, p. 264.

18. Shakespeare, *As You Like It*, II, vii, 167.

19. Harrison, *Prolegomena*, pp. 412–15.

20. Cirlot, pp. 233–34. In numerology seven is symbolic of perfect order and of pain. Nine is the symbol of truth and the three worlds, Heaven, Earth and the Underworld. It is the last in the numerical series before it returns to one or unity.

21. Lemprière, p. 301.

22. Harrison, *Prolegomena*, p. 26.

23. Anton Chekhov, *The Seagull, Chekhov Plays*, trans. Elisaveta Fenn (Middlesex: Penguin, 1954), p. 121.

24. Harding, p. 176.

25. Harding, p. 185. See also Butler, III, 37–38. Elizabeth (Isabella) of Portugal, mother of two, was known as a peacemaker. She forgave her husband King Denis's many infidelities before he died at Santarem, a place name containing the letters of Manresa's surname.

26. Marcus, "Pargeting 'The Pargiters,' " pp. 429, 433.

27. Woolf, "Women and Fiction," *Collected Essays*, II, p. 147. Here Woolf equates the woman artist with the butterfly. In October 1935 Woolf hung a case of butterflies, sent from South America, over the portrait of her "puritan ancestor." The butterflies caused her to think of "the difference between two worlds." See Woolf, *Letters*, V, pp. 438–39.

28. Arnold, p. 54.

29. Richard Ellmann describes Sylvia Beach in quasi-religious terms as a saviour (of Joyce) whom Joyce actually saved by allowing her to publish *Ulysses*. See Ellmann, in Joyce, *Ulysses*, p. 714.

30. Cirlot, p. 150.

31. Woolf, "The Leaning Tower," pp. 148, 179.

32. Graves, *The Greek Myths*, II, index, p. 397.

33. Woolf, "The Leaning Tower," p. 175.

Chapter 4

1. Graves, *The Greek Myths*, I, p. 54.

2. Racine, *Phèdre*, Bartlett, 1, iii, p. 378. "Ce n'est plus une ardeur dans mes veines cachée:/C'est Vénus toute entière à son proie attachée." "It is no longer a passion hidden in my heart:/it is Venus herself fastened to her prey." See Woolf's diary entry for October 2, 1929: "And I shall go in and read *Phèdre*, having picked some apples." *The Diary*, III, p. 259.

3. See, for example, Wyndham Lewis, Chapter V, 'Virginia Woolf,' *Men without Art*, 1934, pp. 158–71, in "An Enemy: Wyndham Lewis," *Virginia Woolf: The Critical Heritage*, p. 336. Lewis describes episodes in Woolf's *Mrs. Dalloway* as "exact and puerile copies" of scenes in Joyce's *Ulysses*.

4. Harding, p. 175.

5. Woolf, *A Room of One's Own*, p. 50.

6. Harding, p. 185.

7. Larousse, pp. 31–32.

8. Harding, p. 174.

9. Arnold, "Dover Beach," l. 35, p. 54.

Afterword

1. Eliot, p. 121.

2. Woolf, *The Diary*, V, p. 278. Eliot, "East Coker," p. 128.

3. Ferdinand de Saussure, quoted in Vincent B. Leitch, *Deconstructive Criticism* (New York: Columbia University Press, 1983), p. 10.

4. Hélène de Cixous quoted in Ann Rosalind Jones, "Writing the Body: Toward an Understanding of L'Ecriture Féminine," *Feminist Studies*, 7 (1981), 252.

5. Virginia Woolf, "Professions for Women," *Virginia Woolf: Women and Writing*, ed. Michèle Barrett (London: The Womens' Press, 1979), p. 62.

6. Woolf, "Craftsmanship," p. 249.

7. Friedrich Nietzsche, quoted in Karl Jaspers, *Nietzsche*, trans. Charles F. Wallroff and Frederick J. Schmitz (Tucson: University of Arizona Press, 1965), p. 227.

8. Muriel Ruykeser, "Kathë Kollwitz," *By A Woman Writt*, ed. Joan Goulianos (Baltimore: Penguin, 1973), p. 337.

9. Tripp, p. 503. See also Lee R. Edwards, "The Labors of Psyche: Toward a Theory of Female Heroism," *Critical Inquiry*, 6 (1979), 33–49.

10. Christiane Rochefort, quoted in Jones, p. 260.

11. Eliot, "Burnt Norton," p. 117.

12. Woolf, *Letters*, II, p. 598.

13. Woolf, "Craftsmanship," pp. 247, 248.

14. Barbara Currier Bell and Carol Ohmann, "Virginia Woolf's Criticism: A Polemical Preface," in Donovan, p. 60, n. 10.

15. Virginia Woolf, *Orlando: A Biography* (New York: Harvest, 1980), p. 266.

16. Harrison, *Prolegomena*, p. 285 and Woolf, *Three Guineas*, p. 6.

17. Emily Dickinson, *The Complete Poems*, ed. Thomas H. Johnson (Toronto: Little, Brown and Company, 1960), 1129, c. 1868, p. 506.

18. Woolf, *A Writer's Diary*, p. 340.

Bibliography

Arnold, Matthew. *Selected Poems,* ed. E.K. Brown. New York: Appleton-Century-Crofts, 1951.

Baring-Gould, Wm. S. and Cecil Baring-Gould, eds. *The Annotated Mother Goose.* New York: Bramhall House, 1962.

Bazin, Nancy Topping. *Virginia Woolf and the Androgynous Vision.* New Jersey: Rutgers University Press, 1973.

Bell, Quentin. *Virginia Woolf: A Biography,* 2 vols. London: Triad/Paladin, 1976.

Berger, John. *About Looking.* New York: Pantheon, 1980.

———. *Ways of Seeing.* Middlesex: Penguin, 1975.

Boyd, Elizabeth French. *Bloomsbury Heritage: Their Mothers and Their Hunts.* New York: Taplinger Publishing Co., 1976.

Briffault, Robert. *The Mothers.* 1927. Abridged Gordon Rattray Taylor. New York: Atheneum, 1977.

Brockett, Oscar G. *History of the Theatre.* Toronto: Allyn and Bacon, Inc., 1977.

Brooke, Rupert. *The Collected Poems of Rupert Brooke: With a Memoir,* ed. E. Marsh. London: Sidgewick and Jackson, 1925.

Bulfinch, Thomas. *Bulfinch's Mythology.* 2 vols. New York: Mentor, 1962.

Butler, Alban. *The Lives of the Saints.* 4 vols. 1758. Ed. Herbert Thurston and Donald Attwater. New York: P.J. Kenedy and Sons, 1963.

Byron, George Gordon, Lord. *The Complete Poetical Works.* Boston: Houghton Mifflin, 1933.

Carpenter, Edward. *The Intermediate Sex.* London: George Allen and Unwin, Ltd., 1908.

Carrington, Dora. *Carrington: Letters and Extracts from her Diaries,* ed. David Garnett. London: Oxford University Press, 1979.

Carroll, Berenice A. "To Crush Him in Our Own Country: The Political Thought of Virginia Woolf." *Feminist Studies,* 4, No. 4 (1978), 99–130.

Casson, Lionel and Eli E. Burriss. *Latin and Greek in Current Use.* New Jersey: Prentice-Hall, 1949.

Chekhov, Anton. *The Seagull, Chekhov Plays.* Trans. Elisaveta Fenn. Middlesex: Penguin, 1954.

Cirlot, J.E. *A Dictionary of Symbols.* Trans. Jack Sage. New York: Routledge and Kegan Paul, Ltd., 1974.

Corrigan, Robert W., ed. *Comedy: A Critical Anthology.* Boston: Houghton Mifflin, 1971.

Curran, Stuart, ed. *Le Bossu and Voltaire on the Epic.* Gainesville: Scholars Facsimiles and Reprints, 1970.

Daly, Mary. *Gyn/Ecology.* Boston: Beacon Press, 1978.

Davenport, Guy. "Joyce's Forest of Symbols," *The Geography of the Imagination.* San Francisco: North Point Press, 1981, pp. 286–99.

Deiman, Werner J. "History, Pattern, and Continuity in Virginia Woolf." In *Virginia Woolf,* ed. Thomas S. W. Lewis, pp. 125–41. New York: McGraw-Hill, 1975.

Di Battista, Maria. *Virginia Woolf's Major Novels: The Fables of Anon.* New Haven and London: Yale University Press, 1980.

Dickinson, Emily. *The Complete Poems,* ed. Thomas H. Johnson. Toronto: Little, Brown and Company, 1960.

Donington, Robert. *Wagner's "Ring" and its Symbols: The Music and the Myth.* New York: St. Martin's Press, 1974.

Donovan, Josephine, ed. *Feminist Literary Criticism: Explorations in Theory.* Lexington: University Press of Kentucky, 1975.

Edel, Leon. *Bloomsbury: A House of Lions.* New York: J.P. Lippincott and Co., 1979.

Edwards, Lee R. "The Labors of Psyche: Toward a Theory of Female Heroism." *Critical Inquiry,* 6, No. 1 (1979), 33–49.

Eliot, George. *The Mill on the Floss,* ed. Gordon S. Haight. Boston: Houghton Mifflin, 1961.

Eliot, T.S. *The Complete Poems and Plays 1909–1950.* New York: Harcourt, Brace & World, 1958.

Fleishman, Avrom. *Virginia Woolf: A Critical Reading.* Baltimore: Johns Hopkins University, 1977.

Forster, E.M. *Virginia Woolf.* New York: Harcourt, Brace & Co., 1942.

Freedman, Ralph, ed. *Virginia Woolf: Revaluation and Continuity.* Berkeley: University of California Press, 1980.

Gilbert, Sandra M. "Costumes of the Mind: Transvestism as Metaphor in Modern Literature." *Critical Inquiry,* 7 (1980), 391-417.

Gilbert, Sandra M. and Susan Gubar. *The Madwoman in the Attic: The Woman Writer and the Nineteenth Century Literary Imagination.* New Haven: Yale University Press, 1979.

Gillespie, Diane Tilby. "Virginia Woolf's Miss La Trobe: The Artist's Last Struggle Against Masculine Values." *Women and Literature,* 5, No. 1 (1977), 38–46.

Goldsmith, Oliver. *She Stoops to Conquer,* ed. Tom Davis. London: Ernest Benn, 1979.

Goulianos, Joan, ed. *By a Woman Writt.* Baltimore: Penguin, 1973.

Graves, Robert. *The Greek Myths.* 2 vols. Middlesex: Penguin, 1973.

––––––– . *The White Goddess.* New York: Farrar, Straus and Giroux, 1980.

Hadden, J. Cuthbert. *The Operas of Wagner.* London: T.C. and E.C. Jack, 1911.

Hall, Nor. *The Moon and the Virgin.* New York: Colophon, 1980.

Harding, M. Esther. *Woman's Mysteries Ancient and Modern.* New York: Harper Colophon, 1971.

Hardwick, Elizabeth. *Seduction and Betrayal: Women and Literature.* New York: Vintage, 1975.

Harrison, Jane Ellen. *Ancient Art and Ritual.* 1918. New York: Greenwood Press, 1969.

––––––– . *Prolegomena to the Study of Greek Religion.* 1908. New York: Meridian, 1960.

––––––– . *Reminiscences of a Student's Life.* London: Hogarth, 1925.

––––––– . *Themis: A Study of the Social Origins of Greek Religion.* 1912. London: Merlin Press, 1963.

Heilbrun, Carolyn G. *Toward a Recognition of Androgyny.* New York: Harper Colophon, 1973.

Holtby, Winifred. *Virginia Woolf: A Critical Memoir.* 1932. Chicago: Cassandra, 1978.

Homans, Margaret. "Eliot, Wordsworth, and the Scenes of the Sisters' Instruction." *Critical Inquiry,* 8, (1981), 223–41.

Jacobus, Mary, ed. *Women Writing and Writing about Women.* New York: Barnes and Noble, 1979.

Jaspers, Karl. *Nietzsche.* Trans. Charles F. Wallroff and Frederick J. Schmitz. Tucson: University of Arizona Press, 1965.

Jones, Ann Rosalind. "Writing the Body: Toward an Understanding of L'Ecriture Féminine." *Feminist Studies,* 7, No. 2 (1981), 247–63.

Joyce, James. *Ulysses.* Harmondsworth: Penguin, 1979.

Jung, Carl C. *Man and His Symbols.* New York: Dell, 1964.

Kaufmann, Walter. *The Portable Nietzsche.* New York: Viking, 1954.

Kenney, Susan M. "Two Endings: Virginia Woolf's Suicide and *Between the Acts.*" *University of Toronto Quarterly,* 4 (1975), 265–89.

Laing, R.D. *The Politics of Experience and The Bird of Paradise.* Middlesex: Penguin, 1977.

Larousse. *World Mythology,* ed. Pierre Grimal. New York: Excalibur, 1981.

Leaska, Mitchell A. *The Novels of Virginia Woolf from Beginning to End.* New York: John Jay Press, 1977.

Lehmann, John. *Thrown to the Woolfs*. New York: Holt, Rinehart and Winston, 1978.

————. *Virginia Woolf and Her World*. London: Thames and Hudson, 1975.

Leitch, Vincent B. *Deconstructive Criticism*. New York: Columbia University Press, 1983.

Lemprière, John. *Lemprière's Classical Dictionary of Proper Names in Ancient Authors*. 1788. London: Routledge and Kegan Paul, Ltd., 1958.

Little, Judy. "Festive Comedy in Woolf's *Between the Acts.*" *Women and Literature*, 5, No. 1 (1977), 26–37.

Llewelyn Davies, Margaret, ed. *Life as We Have Known It*. Intro. V. Woolf. 1932. London: Virago, 1977.

Llewelyn-Davies, Margaret, ed. *Maternity: Letters from Working Women*. 1915. London: Virago, 1978.

Love, Jean O. *Worlds in Consciousness: Mythopoetic Thought in the Novels of Virginia Woolf*. Los Angeles: University of California, 1970.

Majumbar, Robin and Allen McLaurin, eds. *Virginia Woolf: The Critical Heritage*. London: Routledge and Kegan Paul, 1975.

Marcus, Jane, ed. *New Feminist Essays on Virginia Woolf*. Lincoln: University of Nebraska Press, 1981.

————. "'No More Horses': Virginia Woolf on Art and Propaganda." *Women's Studies*, 4, No. 2–3 (1977), 265–90.

————. "Pargeting 'The Pargiters': Notes of an Apprentice Plasterer." *Bulletin of the New York Public Library*, 80, No. 3 (1976–77), 416–35.

————. "Some Sources for *Between the Acts.*" *Virginia Woolf Miscellany*, Winter, 1977.

————. "*The Years* as Greek Drama, Domestic Novel and Gotterdämmerung." *Bulletin of the New York Public Library*, 80, No. 2 (1976–77), 276–301.

Marder, Herbert. *Feminism and Art: A Study of Virginia Woolf*. Chicago: University of Chicago Press, 1968.

Meredith, George. *Diana of the Crossways*. New York: Charles Scribner's Sons, 1910.

Milton, John. *Paradise Lost and Paradise Regained*, ed. Christopher Ricks. New York: Signet, 1968.

Moers, Ellen. *Literary Women*. Garden City: Anchor Books, 1977.

Moore, Madeline. "Virginia Woolf's *The Years* and Years of Adverse Male Reviewers." *Women's Studies*, 4, No. 2–3 (1977), 247–63.

Nicolson, Nigel. *Portrait of a Marriage*. London: Futura, 1978.

Noble, Joan Russell, ed. *Recollections of Virginia Woolf*. Middlesex: Penguin, 1972.

O'Connell, Rev. John P., ed. *The Family Rosary Edition of the Holy Bible*. Chicago: The Catholic Press, 1952.

Opie, Iona and Peter Opie, eds. *The Oxford Dictionary of Nursery Rhymes*. Oxford: The Clarendon Press, 1951.

O[sborne], J[ohn] W. "William Cobbett." *Encyclopaedia Brittanica: Macropaedia*, IV, 1974. 809–10.

Palgrave, Francis Turner, ed. *Palgrave's Golden Treasury*. 1861. London: Oxford University Press, 1926.

Palmer, R.R. and Joel Colton. *A History of the Modern World*. New York: Alfred A. Knopf, 1971.

Patmore, Coventry. *The Angel in the House*. London: George Bell and Sons, 1892.

Pippett, Aileen. *The Moth and the Star*. Toronto: Little, Brown and Co., 1953.

Rich, Adrienne. *Of Woman Born*. New York: Bantam, 1977.

————. *On Lies, Secrets and Silence*. New York: Norton, 1979.

Rigney, Barbara Hill. *Madness and Sexual Politics in the Feminist Novel*. Wisconsin: University of Wisconsin Press, 1978.

Rose, Phyllis. *Woman of Letters*. New York: Oxford University Press, 1978.

Sandars, N.K. *The Epic of Gilgamesh*. Middlesex: Penguin, 1972.

Shakespeare, William. *As You Like It,* ed. T.J.B. Spencer. Middlesex: Penguin, 1968.

———— . *King Lear,* ed. Alfred Harbage. New York: Penguin, 1979.

Showalter, Elaine. *A Literature of Their Own.* Princeton: Princeton University Press, 1977.

Silver, Brenda. "Virginia Woolf and the Concept of Community: The Elizabethan Playhouse." *Women's Studies,* 4, No. 2–3, 1977.

Sophocles. *The Theban Plays.* Trans. E.F. Watling. Middlesex: Penguin, 1978.

Spater, George and Ian Parsons. *A Marriage of True Minds.* New York: Harcourt Brace Jovanovich, 1977.

Spretnak, Charlene. *Lost Goddesses of Early Greece.* Boston: Beacon Press, 1978.

Stewart, Grace. *A New Mythos: The Novel of the Artist as Heroine, 1877–1977.* Vermont: Eden Press, 1979.

Swinburne, Algernon. Vol. I of *Collected Poetical Works.* London: Wm. Heinemann, Ltd., 1924.

Thompson, E.P. *The Making of the English Working Class.* Harmondsworth: Pelican, 1963.

Trevelyan, George MacAulay. *History of England.* London: Longmans, Green and Co., 1939.

Tripp, Edward. *The Meridian Handbook of Classical Mythology.* New York: New American Library, 1970.

Trombley, Stephen. *'All That Summer She Was Mad.'* London: Junction Books, 1981.

Voltaire, *Candide.* Trans. John Butt. Middlesex: Penguin, 1982.

Waite, Arthur Edward. *A New Encyclopedia of Freemasonry.* New York: Weathervane Books, 1970.

Warner, Sylvia Townsend. *The True Heart.* 1928. London: Virago, 1978.

Wells, H.G. *The Outline of History.* New York: Garden City Publishing Co., 1920.

Weston, Jessie L. *From Ritual to Romance.* New York: Anchor, 1957.

Woolf, Leonard. *The Journey Not the Arrival Matters: An Autobiography of the Years 1939–1969.* New York: Harcourt, Brace & World, 1969.

Woolf, Virginia. *Between the Acts.* New York: Harcourt, Brace & Co., 1941. New York: Panther, 1978.

———— . *Books and Portraits,* ed. Mary Lyon. London: Triad/Panther, 1979.

———— . *Collected Essays.* 4 vols. New York: Harcourt, Brace & World, 1967.

———— . *The Common Reader.* 1925. New York: Harvest, 1953.

———— . *The Diary of Virginia Woolf 1915–1919.* Vol. I, ed. Anne Olivier Bell. Middlesex: Penguin, 1977.

———— . *The Diary of Virginia Woolf 1920–1924.* Vol. II, ed. Anne Olivier Bell and Andrew McNeillie. New York: Harcourt Brace Jovanovich, 1980.

———— . *The Diary of Virginia Woolf 1925–1930.* Vol. III, ed. Anne Olivier Bell and Andrew McNeillie. New York: Harcourt Brace Jovanovich, 1981.

———— . *The Diary of Virginia Woolf 1931–1935.* Vol. IV, ed. Anne Olivier Bell and Andrew McNeillie. London: Hogarth, 1982.

———— . *Flush: A Biography.* London: Hogarth, 1933.

———— . *Freshwater.* Harcourt Brace Jovanovich, 1976.

———— . *A Haunted House and Other Stories.* New York: Harcourt, Brace & Company, 1944.

———— . *Jacob's Room.* 1922. New York: Panther, 1979.

———— . *The Flight of the Mind.* Vol. I of *The Letters of Virginia Woolf, 1888–1912,* ed. Nigel Nicolson and Joanne Trautmann. London: Chatto and Windus, 1980.

———— . *The Question of Things Happening.* Vol. II of *The Letters of Virginia Woolf, 1912–1922,* ed. Nigel Nicolson and Joanne Trautmann. London: Chatto and Windus, 1980.

———— . *A Change of Perspective.* Vol. III of *The Letters of Virginia Woolf, 1923–1928,* ed. Nigel Nicolson and Joanne Trautmann. London: Chatto and Windus, 1980.

———— . *A Reflection of the Other Person.* Vol. IV of *The Letters of Virginia Woolf, 1929–1931,* ed. Nigel Nicolson and Joanne Trautmann. London: Chatto and Windus, 1981.

———— . *The Sickle Side of the Moon.* Vol. V of *The Letters of Virginia Woolf, 1932–1935,* ed. Nigel

Nicolson and Joanne Trautmann. London: Chatto and Windus, 1982.

———— . *Leave the Letters Till We're Dead.* Vol. VI of *The Letters of Virginia Woolf, 1936–1941,* ed. Nigel Nicolson and Joanne Trautmann. London: Chatto and Windus, 1983.

———— . *To the Lighthouse.* 1927. New York: Harvest, 1978.

———— . *Mrs. Dalloway.* Intro. Virginia Woolf. New York: Modern Library, 1928.

———— . *Moments of Being,* ed. Jeanne Schulkind. London: Triad/Panther, 1978.

———— . *Orlando: A Biography.* 1928. New York: Harvest, 1980.

———— . *The Pargiters: The Novel-Essay Portion of 'The Years',* ed. Mitchell Leaska. New York: The New York Public Library, 1977.

———— . *A Room of One's Own.* 1929. New York: Panther, 1977.

———— . *Three Guineas.* 1938. Middlesex: Penguin, 1977.

———— . *Virginia Woolf: Women and Writing,* ed. and introd. Michèle Barratt. London: The Women's Press, 1979.

———— . *The Waves.* 1931. New York: Harcourt, Brace & World, 1959.

———— . *A Writer's Diary,* ed. Leonard Woolf. London: Triad/Panther, 1979.

———— . *The Years.* 1937. New York: Panther, 1977.

Woolf, Virginia and Lytton Strachey. *Letters,* ed. L. Woolf and J. Strachey. New York: Harcourt, Brace & Co., 1956.

Wordsworth, William. *Selected Poems,* ed. Walford Davies. London: J.M. Dent, 1975.

Wright, E.M. *The Life of Joseph Wright.* 2 vols. London: Oxford University Press, 1932.

Wright, Joseph, ed. *The English Dialect Dictionary.* 6 vols. London: Oxford University Press, 1961.

Index